2 50

Kenneth H. Korby
St. Louis, Missouri

Theology and Modern Literature

William Belden Noble Lectures, 1956

Theology and Modern Literature

teste David cum Sibylla

Amos N. Wilder

Harvard University Press, Cambridge, 1958

Grateful acknowledgments are due to the publishers and copyright holders for
permission to quote from the following copyrighted material:

"To His Father," from *ROAN STALLION, TAMAR and Other Poems*, by Robin-
son Jeffers, copyright 1924 and renewed 1951 by Robinson Jeffers. "Their Beauty
Has More Meaning," from *THE DOUBLE AXE and Other Poems*, by Robinson
Jeffers, copyright 1947 by Robinson Jeffers. Lines from *DEAR JUDAS and Other
Poems*, by Robinson Jeffers, copyright 1929 and renewed 1957 by Robinson Jeffers.
Lines from *Selected Poetry*, by Robinson Jeffers, copyright 1938 by Robinson Jeffers.
Reprinted by permission of Random House, Inc.
Collected Poetry of W. H. Auden, copyright 1945 by W. H. Auden. *Nones*, by
W. H. Auden, copyright 1951 by W. H. Auden. Reprinted by permission of
Random House, Inc. and Faber and Faber, Ltd.
The Collected Poems of Wallace Stevens, copyright 1950, 1954, by Wallace Stevens.
Reprinted by permission of Alfred A. Knopf, Inc. and Faber and Faber, Ltd.
CEREMONY and Other Poems, by Richard Wilbur (Harcourt, Brace & Co., Inc.),
copyright 1950 by Richard Wilbur.
Collected Poems, by Archibald MacLeish (Houghton Mifflin Company), copyright
1952 by Archibald MacLeish.
Slick But Not Streamlined, by John Betjeman (Doubleday and Company, Inc.),
copyright 1947 by John Betjeman.
Short Is The Time, by C. Day Lewis, copyright 1940, 1943, by Oxford University
Press, New York, Inc. Reprinted by permission of the publisher and Jonathan
Cape, Ltd.
Collected Poems of W. B. Yeats (The Macmillan Company), copyright 1938 by The
Macmillan Company. Reprinted by permission of Mrs. Yeats and Messrs. Macmillan
& Co. Ltd.
The Cock of Heaven, by Elder Olson (The Macmillan Company), copyright 1940
by The Macmillan Company.

Library of Congress Catalog
Card Number 58–11556

Printed in the United States of America

To Robert Henry Pfeiffer
1892–1958

Acknowledgments

The chapters which follow represent, in revised form, the William Belden Noble Lectures, five in number, delivered in the Harvard University Memorial Church in November 1956. This lectureship was established in 1898 by the widow of the clergyman for whom it was named. I am glad to record my appreciation of the opportunity thus afforded under the terms of the foundation to deal in a university setting with aspects of the Christian faith, and for the invitation in this case to relate these to the field of literature. I also wish to express my special debt to my colleague Dr. George A. Buttrick, in whose hands as Preacher to the University and Chairman of the Board of Preachers the appointment resides, as well as to Mrs. Buttrick, for their hospitality and many courtesies in connection with the lectures. My thanks are also due to Mrs. Raymond Wilding-White and to Mrs. Margoret J. Smith for their ready and discerning assistance in the preparation of the manuscript, the former at the time of the lectures and the latter in connection with the present publication.

I have made use at one point of a number of pages prepared as a draft statement for the Division of Religion and the Arts of the National Council of Churches. I have also used a number of pages contributed at one time or another to *Christianity and Crisis,* including the short article, "Artist and Believer," published in October 1953. This article was included in the symposium *What the Christian Hopes for in Society,* edited by Wayne H. Cowan, Association Press, 1957, and I am grateful to the original publishers and to the Association Press for permission to use it. It is here incorporated in the Foreword.

Contents

Theology and Modern Literature

Foreword

There are signs today that the long-standing cleavage between Christianity and the arts is being overcome, and from both sides. On the side of religion we find here and there a new appreciation of aesthetic matters as well as repudiation of sentimental and insipid forms of art too long associated with it. This new artistic sensitivity arises chiefly out of the deepened religious and theological awareness of the churches, one which demands more adequate symbolic expression. It also arises out of contact with the modern arts. For the work of the modern artist, however much of a shock it may at first represent for the religious institutions, ultimately helps to disillusion the believer with respect to his habitual standards of taste and imagination. Moreover, the modern arts reflect the same fundamental crisis which has awakened the church in our time. We therefore find that from the side of the arts also the cleavage in question has been narrowed. A great deal of the most significant art of this century has had striking theological implications, direct and indirect, and this has been abundantly recognized in modern criticism.

A theologian nevertheless must always enter with diffidence into the field of aesthetic and especially literary studies. My concern in this book is chiefly with the latter.

1

It is true that a historian of biblical literature is engaged in the same general kind of task and is constrained by the same disciplines and methods as his colleagues in departments of English, classics, or romance languages. Yet the forms of biblical literature and their whole character and context are so different that a considerable distance separates the biblical scholar from those who are concerned with the humanities in the narrower sense. Something of the same isolation of literary pursuits characterizes the student of the writings of Asia and of the great faiths of the East. Such studies will no doubt go on in relative independence of each other, though we may welcome the achievement of a worker like Erich Auerbach in his relating of biblical and early Christian literature to classical writings. The other side of the problem is seen in the handicaps of the humanistic scholar in dealing with the Scriptures and their heritage, indeed, in the work of any period. Certainly the familiar approach to the Bible "as literature" in English departments has its drawbacks. Teachers trained in humanistic method and on classical and Western models are ill-prepared to deal with the Hebraic-Christian presuppositions wherever they appear, and especially with the Scriptures even when treated as an English classic in the form of the Authorized Version. But this is only to say that there are inevitable hazards wherever there are frontiers to be crossed.

But the diffidence of the theologian with respect to modern literature has an even more considerable occasion. The field of literary criticism has its own highly specialized autonomy. Not only is modern criticism a special discipline, but it moves rapidly. There are many pitfalls for the outsider. I read, for example, in a leading critical review that one of the long-recognized pillars of the whole

edifice of the critics is now to be discarded, namely, Mr.
Eliot's celebrated thesis concerning the "dissociation of
sensibility." The article is fortunately not finally per-
suasive, and I do not find the modern critical achievement
falling apart in other respects, granted its diversity. Yet the
terrain in question is exposed to many cross-fires, and
issues both of rhetoric and of life-attitude are there engaged. In venturing into this subject matter I take some
encouragement from the fact that when Mr. Munroe
Spears took over the editorship of the *Sewanee Review*
he expressed the hope that the time had come when "the
intellectual lion and the clerical lamb might once again
lie down together."

I look on what follows, therefore, as in the nature of a
series of soundings or explorations. There are considerations arising out of modern letters which have interested
me not only as a reader but as theologian. I have selected
certain writers or writings as illustrative. I am aware of
the problem of literature and belief and have no simple
answer to it. I am aware of the didactic fallacy and have
sought to avoid it. I recognize that a work of art is first
of all and always to be understood in its own aesthetic
terms. I am, indeed, persuaded that critics are disposed to
lean over backwards on these issues to safeguard the autonomy of art in a time when it is under all kinds of alien
pressures. I believe, moreover, that all imaginative crea-
tions from the oldest myth and ritual to the most recent
poem have their own kind of declarative or cognitive role,
offer "news of reality." It is in this respect that modern
literature opens itself to theological and moral scrutiny.

A reader of these chapters will note that if there be any
persuasion hidden or otherwise in their contents it is at

least directed as much to the contribution that secular art and thought can make to the faith as it is to the contrary theme. I am interested in the example afforded to the believer by the artist. The church today can learn not only from the work of the modern artist but also and especially from his calling and way of life. To this aspect of their mutual relation the remainder of this preface will be devoted.

The life of the artist offers many analogies to the life of faith. The strictness of his way of life, the combination of ascesis and joy, the law of incarnation which limits all false spirituality, such features of the artist's calling carry both rebuke and instruction for the Christian, especially in a time when indulgence and unreality have infected the practice of religion. In today's cultural disarray, moreover, the modern literary artist in particular has much to teach us bearing on the rediscovery of meaning, the sifting of traditions, the discernment of spirits, and the renewal of the word. The problem of communication for the church today is no less urgent than for the artist. Our elaboration of a new grammar and rhetoric of faith and apologetic can learn much from the new discourse of the poets.

Consider the following passage from Rilke's *Les Cahiers de Malte Laurids Brigge,* which may be taken as a parable of the religious life and of the fruit it may bear, of how greatness comes to birth. The young Brigge has written some poetry. Yet, he observes, how little poetry amounts to when written in youth. After a long life, yes, at its very end, after all the buffeting and the myriad and cumulative situations and confrontations — then perhaps one could write ten good lines of verse. For poetry is not constituted by sentiments (those, indeed, come early enough) but by life-experiences.

To write a single line one must have seen many cities,
men and things . . . One must have had the memory of the
groans of child-birth, and of the pale and sleeping forms of
those who have given birth, their bodies now disburdened.
One must also have been with the dying, have watched by
the dead with the window open to the sounds of the world's
stir outside. And it is not enough to have memories. . . .
It is only when within us they have become blood, outlook,
gesture, when they no longer have any name and are in-
distinguishable from ourselves, it is only then in some
rare unexpected moment, out of all this, that the first
word of a poem may arise.[1]

This testimony of a great poet offers its clues for the
believer. For neither is religion constituted of sentiments.
Life is full of sentiments, lavish, potent, and exquisite.
But they are not the important thing. Many no doubt
confuse them with true spirituality. Indeed, because they
are rebuffed in seeking them in the Christian religion they
take umbrage and avoid those churches where something
more austere is demanded and offered. Or they form their
own cenacles and elaborate their own cults where trite
poetizings or unashamed heart throbs or tenuously masked
passion itself may with some success pretend to fulfill the
role of faith and its utter venture as it wrestles with God.

We need to be aware of the high price of religious faith,
and not confuse it with the various aspects and talents of
the inner life available to all comers. The analogy of
poetry warns us that sentiments, emotions, memories, are
but raw ingredients. Sentiments must be proved in life,
"experiences" must be digested, emotions and memories
must fade and again come to life in character. Then, perhaps, by an unrecognized gestation, a richer and deeper
self having taken form, a true prayer may voice itself

[1] Paris: Éditions Émile-Paul Frères, 1926, pp. 25–26.

within us. Under favoring conditions a veil may suddenly be torn aside disclosing the true nature of our human situation, and an impulse toward the love of our fellow creatures arise too majestic to dissipate, as do our common benevolences, under the tests of life. Unless some such maturing has taken place, some such price be paid, we are not in a position to recognize the signs and works and wonders of grace or to read with understanding the special rhetoric of faith as we find it in the Scriptures.

All this means selection, rejection, isolation, conflict for the believer as for the artist. The most elementary of all rules here — peculiarly offensive to the standing mores of our democratic outlook, where the truth that one man is as good as another is extended to condone mediocrity and to isolate and handicap excellence — this most elementary of all rules is that "a man must break with the existing order of the world and with its interests and values." This demand, which is a truism for the genuine artist, only echoes with varying depths of context the peremptory summons of Jesus to his disciples that found such frequent utterance: "Go, sell whatsoever thou hast . . ." "Seek first the kingdom of God and his righteousness." And the new sphere, not of indemnification but rather of surpassingly lavish surpluses of discovery and satisfaction opened up, here and now in this age, is similarly indicated in the special symbols of the time: "There is no man that hath left house, or brethren, or sisters, or father, or mother, or wife, or children, or lands, for my sake, and for the gospel's, but he shall receive an hundred-fold now in this time, houses, and brethren, and sisters, and mothers, and children, and lands, with persecutions."

The analogy of the artist suggests, indeed, both the cost and the rewards of real devotion. For while on the one hand he makes himself, as it were, an Ishmaelite and a eunuch among men through the single-mindedness and intensity with which he pursues a special province among life's many offerings, on the other hand he achieves a sensibility and a wealth and mastery in that province incommensurable with the common experience. He slowly builds up an unseen edifice of sensibility, a coral reef in the soul of significances and relationships, a house not made with hands of images and imaginings — an edifice wrought indeed out of the common realities, but set in new relations, bathed in the light of the imagination, transfigured not into a false unreality but into their true significance. Thus what began with the daily dust of life and the precisely observed fact of time and sense is now recognized to be a city let down from heaven.

If such a harvest after such a sowing — whether of the artist or the Christian — appears strange, difficult, profitless to the man who has taken few steps outside the beaten path, or who has denied himself little, it is not a matter for surprise. These compensations are for the resolute and the reckless. There are those who sally forth toward discovery and achievement, but who, nevertheless, are careful to keep their communications with their base. Their life as men or artists is made up of a shuttling back and forth between the secure and the hazardous. They are commuters between the old and the new, between the sown land and the frontier. The new perspectives are not firmly grasped. But to enter into the new horizons calls for a decisiveness of repudiation and relinquishment, for a certain ascetic strain of grimness. Yet out of the tension and discipline arises a greater joy, as "out of the strong came forth sweetness."

A modern poet has well stated the fateful hesitation, the

clinging to wonted images, which disqualify us for a wider
range of awareness. The parable is specially apt for a time
of cultural crisis like our own, where old securities
whether of faith or "way of life" are undermined. We may
prefix to the poem the remark of Rilke: "They would so
love to dwell among the signs and meanings that have
become precious to them." C. Day Lewis, in his poem
"Questions," shows us how easily we let ourselves be "immobilized" by present seductions which we nevertheless
recognize for what they are.

How long will you keep this pose of self-confessed
And aspen hesitation
Dithering on the brink, obsessed
Immobilized by the feminine fascination
Of an image all your own,
Or doubting which is shadow, which is bone?

Will you wait womanish, while the flattering stream
Glosses your faults away?
Or would you find within that dream
Courage to break the dream, wisdom to say
That wisdom is not there?
Or is it simply the first shock you fear?

Do you need the horn in your ear, the hounds at your heel,
Gadflies to sting you sore,
The lightning's angry feint, and all
The horizon clouds boiling like lead, before
You'll risk your javelin dive
And pierce reflection's heart, and come alive? [2]

There is one further analogy in the work of the artist,
particularly of the modern artist, that is worthy of attention here. We may illustrate by the foregoing poem. Real-

[2] "Questions" from *Short Is the Time* by C. Day Lewis, Oxford University Press, 1945, p. 29.

ity, we have intimated, whether in terms of art or faith, is difficult of attainment. This difficulty inheres also inevitably in the language of genuine art and faith. It is always difficult for us to come alive to that which is beyond us, because it involves death in some measure. The language and symbols of that which is beyond us or new to us are strange until we have lived the new experience, entered into the new relations. If we find the words of Shakespeare or the Bible clear, it is often because we short-cut and shortchange the sense; though to the degree that we have lived the experience and perspective in question we have insight.

The modern arts are difficult because they proceed out of the changed sensibility and experience of our time. The special images, subtleties, and concern of a modern poem like the one quoted above belong to the modern consciousness, and the significance of the poem is only open to those who have known something of the costs involved in the changing moral and psychological patterns of our day. The difficulty of the best modern art is the difficulty of the observer not of the artist. If the observer or reader has not evaded the modern spiritual situation, or lived on its margin, if he has been responsibly concerned with the deeper dilemmas and anguish, public and intimate, of our century, and has had some perception of the nature of art, he will find that the modern poet or artist speaks to him.

But here we have an analogy of the far richer complex of the Christian consciousness and its grammar and thesaurus. Faith has its own rhetoric, and spiritual things are not only spiritually discerned but are reported in a spiritual tongue. This is not to draw a fixed line between spirit and flesh, or between supernatural and natural. For all that is spiritual is first and indeed always in a sense natural. The language of faith may, however, be difficult and strange because we have not lived through the costs that illuminate it. It is a question of where we live and to what we respond. The artist has paid his price and offers his vision of the world to those who have to some degree followed him. The modern artist of our world under judgment has exposed his nerves and heart to the fury and desolation of these decades, and can provide meaning for those who have the same initiation. To those who come to the Gospel and the Scriptures, not with a "wealth of sentiments" or a "success story" of immunities achieved, but with a heart exercised in responsibilities, the veiled symbols of vocation and promise will be as their native tongue.

Chapter I

Religious Dimensions
in Modern Literature

Now that it has come of age, the world is
more godless, and perhaps it is for that very
reason nearer to God than ever before.
> Dietrich Bonhoeffer, in a letter from
> a concentration camp, July 18, 1944

Thus it is precisely the loss of all sacral
features in our civilization which has occasioned
the resurgence among many today of a primitive sense of the sacred.
> P.-R. Régamey, *L'Art Sacré au*
> *XXe Siècle*

There are many signs today of a renewed conversation between Christianity and the arts. These chapters will be largely concerned with this development and its significance. One has the impression sometimes that this dialogue takes on the character of a monologue in the sense that the theologian and the modern artist are saying the same thing. The human situation in our century has deepened both religion and art and brought them nearer together. For an epigraph to this volume we have taken the words from the *Dies Irae*: "Teste David cum Sibylla." The muses sacred and profane agree. There is even a strange appropriateness today in this text from the *Dies Irae*. For in that great mediaeval hymn the common witness of David and the Sibyl is directed to the signs of the times and of an apocalyptic time.

While our chief interest in these discussions will be given to literature, the whole question of religion and the arts is involved. In our first two chapters we shall widen our field accordingly. The ambiguous relation of Christianity to the aesthetic life is a matter of perennial

13

interest. The attitudes of Protestantism in this field, changing with changing circumstances, are of particular interest. The creative tension between religion and the general culture is always sharply reflected in the situation of the arts. This field is therefore highly illuminating for any understanding of our times.

If we start with a recognition of the wide gulf that has, at least until recently, separated the church and the arts, we can give attention to the ways in which this cleavage is being overcome. This first chapter, after some consideration of the situation, will deal with this dialogue from the side of literature and the arts. The second chapter will deal with it from the side of the church, and will assess the quickened interest in the arts evident today among theologians and churchmen. First, however, some prefatory considerations.

1. Christianity and the Arts: The Historic Divorce

The theologian today reminds himself of the historic role served by the church in the fostering of the art forms of the West, and laments the divorce that has ensued, and the radical secularization, for example, of the drama. Protestant theologians, especially those of Calvinist Puritan background, have great searchings of heart as they recall an unflattering history of iconoclasm and asceticism. Theologians write books today about Christianity and culture and about religious symbols. A symposium is projected on *Theology and Literary Criticism*. On the other hand, among art critics and teachers of literature, we find recurrent discussion of such themes as Poetry and Belief, Art and Ritual, Ikon and Idea. Bridges are being thrown across the gulf that separates the church and the modern artist, from both sides, and sometimes they appear to meet.

If we speak of a gulf between religion and the arts today, we should realize that we are dealing with a very complex matter. Distinctions should certainly be made. There is, of course, a great deal of religious art produced today of one kind or another. Almost a billion dollars a year is spent in this country for the construction of new churches. The divergencies of taste in the general population are reflected in the varying quality of the religious paintings, statues, stained glass, and hymnals found in churches, church schools, and Christian homes throughout the country. Unfortunately, it is in good part this Christian art itself which has alienated the true artist.

When we speak of the cleavage between religion and the arts, we usually have in mind the whole modern period, and we contrast this period with the Middle Ages, when the arts were the handmaidens of the church. A recent attempt in Nottingham, England, to renew the local version of the mediaeval miracle plays, which had lapsed for hundreds of years, succeeded only in highlighting the changed spirit of our modern secular culture. The relation of the ancient guild, craft, or corporation to such Christian mysteries was something not reproducible today in the modern labor union, chamber of commerce, bar association, or even the local authors' club or drama league. Very likely, a more spontaneous and general response would have been secured from the twentieth-century city of Nottingham if the Committee on Rites and Ceremonies had gone even farther back, and had resurrected a chariot race. As a matter of fact, the modern Olympic Games furnish a direct link with an age when

religion and art were unified. Certainly the bullfight in
Spain has still a significant, if indirect, relation to the
ancient cult of Mithra, in its deep impact on the Iberian
audience, as Henri de Montherlant has so strikingly
brought out in his early novel *Les Bestiaires*.

Evidently one has to go far afield to identify any really
deep, organic relation today between religion and art in
a communal or civic sense, in a sense which would include the economic life as well as the strictly religious.
Of course, one finds something of this in Catholic civic
ceremonies in Latin lands, as in non-Christian cultures.
D. H. Lawrence tried to work out his dream of such a
sacral order of life in his novel *The Plumed Serpent*,
but myth and ritual are not so easily extemporized, even
on paper. We live in a world which calls for the separation of church and state, despite various ceremonial survivals, and the separation of religion and the arts is of a
piece with this truncated culture.

It will be urged that we should speak rather of the
separation of Protestantism and the arts, yet Roman
Catholics today are as much concerned with the problem
as are Protestants. Catholic protests against the art objects
of St. Sulpice (*la bondieuserie*) are as vehement as are
protests among discerning Protestants against the religious
chromos and "beauty-parlor" Christs which are so ubi-
quitous in our churches. The dilemma of Catholic art
is reflected in the attitude of the modern Catholic saint
Léon Bloy, who, as Wladimir Weidlé puts it, "reviling
art, as it were stripped it off from his body like a sordid
garment, to prostrate himself naked at the foot of the
Cross." [1] But the more characteristic tendency of French
Catholics is to call upon the modern artist to correct the
artificiality and vacuity of the prevailing taste. And here

we have the setting for the extensive controversy that has
gone on over the Matisse chapel at Vence, the church at
Azy, and other bold initiatives. Weidlé, a Catholic critic,
laments what one meets with among believers on the Con-
tinent, a "perfect indifference to art, and among the
artists a crass ignorance with respect to the import of the
Christian faith." [2]

The real problem, evidently, is that of the alienation
of the artist and the creative writer from the Christian
tradition as a whole. On the one hand, their gifts have
not been available to the church in the service of the
ecclesiastical arts. But more significant still, much of the
really creative work of the modern age has not been inspired by, or oriented to, Christian presuppositions. It can
be objected here that the artist, as artist, is not concerned
with a religious confession one way or the other. Yet the
fact remains that many of the most talented and influential artists of the nineteenth and twentieth centuries have
represented not only a detachment from, but often a clear
disaffection with, the religious traditions of the West.

2. The Christian Idealist Tradition

Now one can, indeed, point to a Christian romantic or
idealist tradition in English and American writers of the
period which runs through the Victorian age down
through the Georgian poets to the present day. There
would seem to be no breach between Christianity and
art in this stream, which would include painters like
the pre-Raphaelites and poets like Browning, Francis
Thompson, Masefield, and Vachel Lindsay. It is this
tradition which consciously or unconsciously dominates

the attitudes of hosts of men and women today, particularly in the churches. It represents a religious and cultural outlook which has had glorious antecedents, and which still has a vital substance for those strata which have not yet been corroded by the acids of modernity.

But this entente between Christianity and art is today deeply compromised. So far as its theology is concerned, this Christian version of romantic idealism shares in the disaster that has overtaken philosophical idealism generally. Robert and Elizabeth Browning, like Ruskin, Charles Kingsley, and others, represented a very real bridge between Christianity and the arts, not only for their own age, but for many readers ever since. They still can make that claim. But the climate has radically changed. The new generations of our century cannot accept the axioms which they presupposed and are not reached by the idiom in which they spoke. This is not to disparage the stature of Browning or of Dickens or of Tennyson. In fact, the real attitude of many moderns to such writers is one of wistfulness rather than scorn. It is often said that the modern mood finds an insufficient sense of evil in the Christian Victorian writers, and, indeed, in the romantic poets. This is not the whole story. Lionel Trilling has shown how unflinching a sense of the fatalities of life was possessed by Keats. It is true that we no longer share the confidence in progress held by the Victorians. But Browning's voice becomes dim today, not only for these ideological reasons. It is, rather, a matter as we say of his sensibility. His experience of life, his formation, and his consequent idiom are too foreign to our life.

The Christian idealist tradition has become attenuated in our time, both because of this change in sensibility and because of the new tragic experiences of our century; and the two are no doubt related. We find many of the older Christian poets and artists wanting, both in theology and in aesthetics. If we turn back to the nineteenth century, we go to G. M. Hopkins rather than to Browning; to Dostoievsky rather than to Dickens; to Emily Dickinson rather than to the American "household poets." We find aesthetic justification for this. But we also find a greater sense of reality, of things as they are, in the writers preferred. It is not only that they are more aware of evil, but that their awareness of good likewise carries more authenticity for us.

It is such considerations as these which explain the weaker hold today of religious poets who were highly cherished only a generation or two ago. It is recognized today that the Catholic idealism of Francis Thompson had sideslipped very far toward a secular aestheticism. The platonic idealism of Robert Bridges was seemingly unable to digest enough of the raw ingredients of human experience to achieve greater artistic stature. Vachel Lindsay is dated as an apostle, though certainly not as a troubadour.

In this brief glance at what we have called the idealist tradition we have no doubt begged many questions. The problem before us is that of the gulf between religion and the arts. The legacy of the American "household poets," so far as it is alive, offers us an exception, as does the Victorian tradition. We distinguish between this common tradition as it exists today and the gifted writers of the nineteenth century. The latter have been unduly disparaged; under the conditions of our *Zeitgeist* we have been disqualified from any fair appreciation of them. This injustice, indeed, is now in course of correction.

But this legacy as we know it today, whether in England
or America, is not vital or relevant enough to reconcile
Christianity and the modern arts. The fact is that the
"traditional artist," as we know him today, or the "traditional poet," is not traditional enough.

Our negative judgment on the recent idealist tradition
should not be identified with that of those theological
critics today who indict in a wholesale way the romantic
and transcendentalist heresies of the nineteenth century.
The middle-class religious sentimentalism and moralism
which are our chief targets lacked significant religious
depth because they forfeited immediacy of relation both
with God and with nature. The somewhat astringent modern arts could benefit by more and not less of the ample
romantic breath. Even theologically considered, there
may be as much heresy in anti-romantic ascetic Christianity as there is in Wordsworth or Shelley. The Christian
doctrine of creation is the chief casualty in contemporary
theological movements, whether neo-orthodox or existentialist.

Resistance to the modern movements in the arts today
comes especially from a public brought up in the roman-
tic-idealist tradition. This resistance also unfortunately
blocks the best contemporary efforts to purify religious
art. This public appeals either to a Christian idealism,
suggested by such figures as we have named, or to a more
general religious mysticism, identified with "A.E.,"
Tagore, the early Yeats, or Khalil Gibran. For such readers there is no cleavage between religion and the arts,
because the Holy Spirit is identified with the Muse. We
grant that the Holy Spirit and the Muse are not finally
unrelated; but what these idealists fail to recognize is that
the Muse, as they understand her, is far from being the

same Muse as that invoked of old. Their Muse, as an inspirational impulse, is a diminishing echo of the nineteenth-century romantic Muse, who had herself been rudely exiled and sequestered from the main business of the industrial age. Her domain had been increasingly confined to that of dreams, sentiments, and aspirations. Beauty became a special precinct, rather than the transfiguration of the actual world itself. Unfortunately, also, the worst forms of religious art and poetry created in this tradition are to be found today in what is known as Sunday-School art, in "gospel hymns," and in sentimental religious paintings.

D. H. Lawrence, writing of the hymns which he had known in Nottinghamshire, speaks of "the ghastly sentimentalism that came like a leprosy over religion." [3] Lawrence was not hypercritical. He spoke his admiration of the Bristol hymnbook, which he had used as a child, and of what he called "healthy hymns." But he had an innate sense for the specious and the meretricious. The reality of Christian worship cannot be restored by injections of saccharine. Paul Claudel pillories this procedure: "If the salt hath lost its savour, wherewith shall it be salted? *With sugar!*" This would appear to be a widespread prescription. But this kind of religion and this kind of art represent a dead end. Christian inspirational and moralistic art strive to recapture the great afflatus which the romantic movement, especially transcendentalism, possessed at its height. It only succeeds, however, in voicing an echo of an echo. It is better to recognize that religion and art are completely divorced than to insist on this kind of marriage of the two, for the kind of art it favors is precisely what alienates the true artist from religion.

Any true bridge-building between religion and the arts will require a deeper grasp of what religion is and what art is: a better theology and a better aesthetic. A better theology will not identify religion or Christianity with any and every inspirational or didactic impulse, nor with any and every experience of Beauty or the Spirit. And a better aesthetic will not be satisfied with a view of the imagination which exiles it from the real world, from the World's Body, to use Ransom's phrase.

It has been possible for modern romantics to unite religion and art because they were both romantic. When religion and poetry become ivory-tower activities — when they are exiled from the business of the world — when religion is assigned to a shrine and poetry to a pedestal, they console themselves by becoming confederates. Shrine religion becomes aestheticism. Pedestal art takes on a pseudo-sanctity.

But when religion and art are rebaptized in a total life-experience they are first divided according to their distinct roles, and then may be drawn into a really valid interrelation and interpenetration.

3. Literature and the Modern Crisis

A discussion between theologian and artist or critic is possible at a new level today just because both Christianity and the arts have been affected and deepened by the forces of our period. Some of the great fruitful polar tensions of Western culture are again worthy of exploration, such tensions as are suggested by the contrasts: Jerusalem and Athens, David and the Sibyl, Christ and Dionysus. At least the dialogue between religion and the arts today represents more than the mere superficial hostility suggested by the terms Zion and Bohemia. We are in a position today where the secular art critic will find much of importance bearing on aesthetics in the work of an older Christian writer like Kierkegaard, or a more recent one, like Paul Tillich; and the systematic theologian finds himself addressed by novelists like Kafka and Faulkner, or by a poem like Robert Penn Warren's *Brother to Dragons*.

Let us try to suggest the many-sided confrontation of religion and the arts today. Most significant is the transformation of the arts themselves in the twentieth century. Consider many of the most significant modern writers and artists, and many of the most significant older figures whose reputations have been revived: we note in most cases such features as the break with verism or with naturalism; surrealist and nonrepresentational style; metaphysical or existential or apocalyptic concern; a wrestling with problems of good and evil, of bondage and redemption. One may cite here the words of Weidlé, who speaks of an irresistible attraction toward religious concerns which operates upon the modern writer. "By comparison with the last century, ours almost takes on the character of a century of faith." He continues by noting that the prominence assumed by writers who are believers and by religious themes in the literature of Europe and America is infinitely greater than was the case fifty or sixty years ago.[4] The English poet John Heath-Stubbs says much the same thing in his introduction to the *Faber Book of Twentieth-Century Verse*.

> It is the theme of personal relationships on which, increasingly, the poets of our century have laid the most stress. For it is against the survival of personal and human values that the odds in our mass-civilization have been laid.

But these pressures have driven the poets to the rediscovery
of emotional, mythopoeic, and ultimately, of religious
modes of response to the world. The religious preoccupations of so many twentieth-century poets would probably
have surprised their grandparents.[5]

No doubt it is misleading to characterize works of the
imagination in terms of theme or content. Nevertheless,
for the moment let us look at the matter from this confessedly partial point of view. We can find some temporary
justification when we recall how many critics have used
a poem like Yeats' "The Second Coming" not merely for
an aesthetic discussion, but as a kind of cultural document;
or have discussed the novels of Kafka, not to mention
those of Malraux or Silone, in a social context; or have
drawn connections between such paintings as those of
Dali, Chirico, Braque, and a supposed dissolution of an
older kind of personal consciousness; or have pointed to
D. H. Lawrence's analogous disgust with an outworn conception of plot and character belonging to a static and
devitalized social order. There is surely some validity in
making such cultural inferences from the work of the
artist, or identifying particular social judgments implicit
in poem or novel.

When, for example, a poet fires such repeated and
heavy broadsides against Puritan New England at all
periods as Robert Lowell does in his work there is no
alternative but to recognize that the poet expresses a
personal view, that the poetry contains a dogmatic element which can be paraphrased.[6] The mistake lies in iso-
lating observations of this order from the final aesthetic
judgment on the work in question. Any social or religious
meaning that a novel or poem may have is finally to be
defined in terms of the work as a whole.

With this kind of qualification in mind, let us return to our canvass of the features of modern art which suggest a religious dimension. We need not dwell upon the work of such figures as Eliot, Auden, Claudel, Fry, and others, much of whose work is clearly identifiable with a Christian standpoint. More significant is the moral and metaphysical element in highly influential modern writers not identified with formal religion. One can well say that the deeper moral and spiritual issues of man today are often more powerfully canvassed by such writers than by theologians themselves. Without ceasing to be artists, such writers are often also lay prophets, uncanonical witnesses, who in the default of the official church are constrained to explore the enigmas of life and conduct as best they can. A great deal of contemporary theology sounds thin, repetitive, and abstract when set beside the brilliant psychological and moral observation and the historical reflection which one can find in the best of the little magazines today. With all their error, the immediate, sensitive wrestling with modern circumstances of a Joyce or a Gide or a William Carlos Williams can have a unique authenticity. Thus we may see a long line of modern agnostics or rebels, from Blake and Shelley, Whitman and Melville, to D. H. Lawrence, Kafka, Yeats, and many others, as a kind of lay order in Christendom, engaged in tasks which the official church has not yet fully encountered or assumed. The best of them should be distinguished from the plethora of false prophets and cultists, which abound in an age like ours. We live in what has been called an "age of magicians," and the modern mass public is vulnerable to what Auden has called the "woozier religions," as well as to totalitarian frenzies.

We may well note a few examples of the religious

dimensions of interests in modern writers. We turn first
to D. H. Lawrence. The new dialogue between Christianity and the arts is well illustrated by the appreciative
study of Lawrence by a member of an Anglican religious
order, writing under the name of Father William Tiverton. In a foreword to this work, T. S. Eliot writes:

> [Lawrence's] strictures upon Christianity . . . are often ill-
> informed; at other times they go straight to the heart of
> the matter: and no Christian ought to feel sure that he is
> religious-minded enough to ignore the criticism of a man
> who, without being a Christian, was primarily and always
> religious.[7]

D. H. Lawrence said many things about religion. But
on one point he consistently witnesses against a chief
modern heresy of the church: its false spirituality. Lawrence asserts over and over the Resurrection of the Body.
He reproaches the church for subordinating the Resurrection of Christ to his death and wounds.

> Surely Christ rose with healed hands and feet, sound and
> strong and glad? Surely the passage of the Cross and the
> tomb was forgotten? But no — always the memory of the
> wounds, the smell of the grave-clothes? A small thing was
> the Resurrection, compared with the Cross and the death,
> in this cycle.[8]

Lawrence may miss the full relation of the Cross and
Resurrection, but he rightly protests against the "lilies of
the resurrection," "pale with a deathly scent," which
too often suggest and exhaust the meaning of Easter for
Christians. This writer's point here is related to his
central emphasis, the eternal significance of man's em-
bodied life.

Or take the case of Kafka. This writer's obsessive parables evoke not only a particular cultural suffocation, but

through this they evoke aspects of the human condition itself. If the modern reader is often betrayed by the King James Version into reading the Book of Job as a cento of elegiac and resonant poems, let him read *The Trial* and *The Castle*. In this way he will recover a sense of the stony impasses by which true faith must be measured. To suggest the deeper background of Kafka's outlook, we cite his reply to a questioner who asked him what he made of Christ:

> He is an abyss filled with light. One must close one's eyes if one is not to fall into it. . . . I try to be a true attendant upon grace. Perhaps it will come, perhaps it will not come. Perhaps the quiet yet unquiet waiting is the harbinger of grace, perhaps it is grace itself. I do not know.[9]

Or take the case of Faulkner. We note in Faulkner not only an exploration of social morbidity and its mechanisms, but also the pressure upon these of eternal restorative factors; and we note what Robert Penn Warren calls "the human effort to find or create values in the mechanical round of existence." Faulkner has built part of his work expressly upon the Christ-drama, not only in *The Fable*, but in other novels.

4. Theology and Literary Criticism

The emergence of theological issues in modern criticism should also be recognized. No one proposes to deal with such figures as Hawthorne, Emerson, or Emily Dickinson today without a full knowledge of New England theology and of Puritan moral patterns. No one can do justice to William Blake or, for that matter, to Henry James, father and son, without acquaintance with Sweden-

borg. Understanding of Dostoievsky requires initiation
into the elaborate world of Eastern Orthodoxy. Right
discriminations about G. M. Hopkins require acquaintance with the Scotist wing of Catholic theology. To
read Gide requires acquaintance with the Reformed
Church in France, and to read Bernanos or Mauriac calls
for backgrounds in the Gallic tradition and Jansenism.
For the French existentialist novelists, one must know
Kierkegaard. It is a truism that one cannot read Eliot
properly without exploring various religious backgrounds
suggested, for example, in the notes to *The Waste Land*.
Austin Warren in *Rage for Order* has documented a wide
variety of esoteric religious factors which illuminate the
works of Yeats.

Our colleagues in departments of English have often
sent their students to us in the theology classrooms to
get at least some rudimentary knowledge of the chief
figures and episodes in the Bible. How could they read
Milton, Dryden, or Blake if they could not place such
allusions as Lucifer, Ahithophel, Athaliah, Sodom and
Gomorrah, or Susanna? But of late the humanities fac-
ulties are perforce teaching courses in English Calvin-
ism or New England theology or in eighteenth-century
evangelicalism. If a student cannot handle Racine without a knowledge of Jansenism, or Lessing without a
knowledge of the new biblical criticism of his time, how
can he read Milton's *Paradise Lost* without reading the
De Doctrina Christiana? And how is he to decide as to the
supposed heresy in either if he does not know the various strands in the English Reformation? The time is
gone when Milton could be read for his "purple passages"
and when students could ignore the theological structure
of *Paradise Lost* as not relevant to the work of art. How

can the student assess *Samson Agonistes* without some
such analysis of the biblical interpretation of the time,
and the current treatment of the Samson Cycle as afforded
in a book like Michael Krouse's *Milton's Samson and the
Christian Tradition?* [10]

The time is past when literary appreciation could slight
the theological aspects of the work of art, as though all
such elements were external. It is true that crticism today
properly refuses to dissociate any such ideological element
from the total work, but its presence is seriously treated.
It is important to note that the theological aspects of
literature and art bear on the very substance of the work,
on the literary form and style. We might suppose, for
example, that the work of Rabelais would only be topi-
cally related to Christianity. The fact is that we miss the
point about his mixed style unless we relate it to late
mediaeval preaching and to the author's Franciscan youth.

Another way to bring out the religious involvement of
the modern artist and critic would be to study the particular ancient myths or fables employed in modern works.
The artist uses them to come to grips with the human con-
stants, with perennial givens in an age of unbelief. The
modern man is confronted, in the words of R. W. B.
Lewis, "by a swarm of conflicting vocabularies — rival
accounts of human nature and human destiny, the religious and psychological and all the others." [11] But a dis-
trust of all such public languages leads the writer "to
resort more and more to fables, gestures and parables."
Such utilization of symbolic patterns is a way of identifying meaning and coherence in human experience, and of
binding together ancient and modern times. But as
Wallace Fowlie has said of Baudelaire's concern to discover order where chaos exists: "What is of order must

of necessity be spiritual." Moreover, the myths or ancient
vehicles so used commonly carry with them still an aura
of transcendent reference: myths of fertility and renewal;
myths of guilt and expiation; myths of judgment and
apocalypse. One could add a long list of lesser patterns,
whose quasi-religious significance is apparent: the motif
of the explorer (MacLeish's *Conquistador*); or of the
innocent who passes through many initiations into experience (Henry James' *The Princess Cassamassima*); or
of the initiate who journeys through the underworld
(*Joseph in Egypt*); the motif of the prodigal son (which
recurs in Robinson Jeffers); the motif of migrations of
tribes and of builders of cities (the *Anabase* of St.-John
Perse); the motif of lost and found or departure and
return (the theme of Orpheus or that of the Phoenix);
motifs of epiphany and metamorphosis (Cocteau's *Blood
of a Poet* and *Beauty and the Beast*), in one way or another suggesting levels at which our natural categories of
time, space, causation, and identity are dissolved in favor
of a more dynamic grasp of existence. The reader can fill
in the names of modern writers who have used such particular vehicles of generic import.

In a paper on "Religious Symbols in Contemporary
Literature," [12] Professor Nathan A. Scott, Jr., has classified
the symbols in question under four heads. There is, first,
the myth of the Isolato. Scott takes the term from *Moby
Dick,* and offers such examples as Joe Christmas in Faulk-
ner's *Light in August,* and the estranged protagonists of
Kafka. Second, there is the myth of Hell or "distance from
God," with allusions made to *The Waste Land* and to
Sartre's *No Exit.* In the third place, there is the myth of
voyage, or of the quest, with illustrations taken from the
Four Quartets. Finally, there is the myth of sanctity, illus-

trated by the interest of modern writers in figures like St. Joan of Arc and Becket, or in vicarious sufferers like *Billy Budd* or the central protagonists in Faulkner's *Fable* and his *Requiem for a Nun.*

Another way to note the religious depth of the modern artistic situation is to examine the figures of the past who have enjoyed notable revivals of prestige and influence in the twentieth century. Strictly aesthetic factors can hardly be isolated in explaining the appeal today of Blake, Hoelderlin, Dostoievsky, Melville, and others. The interest in Blake fits with the modern dilemma of reason and imagination, not merely as an academic matter, but as a crux of our human knowing. The interest in Hoelderlin suggests the modern effort to overcome German idealism, and to move beyond the culture symbols of Prometheus and Dionysus to that of Christ. The interest in Dostoievsky, as in Hawthorne (or, for that matter, in the paintings of Brueghel and Bosch), fits with the modern sense of the daemonic, the phenomenon of possession, and the demand for the exorcism of evil powers.

The self-understanding sought by contemporary man requires cultural images: requires, that is, works of art; philosophy and theology as rational disciplines are not adequate to it. The significance of the chief phases of modern history is best found in the creative artistic movements of the period, but the significance of the works produced is not fully brought out by the usual literary-historical or aesthetic studies. Just as our appreciation of myth and ritual in ancient cultures bursts the usual methods pursued by historians of religion, so our understanding of the major symbols in modern literature requires an approach which transcends the usual procedures of literary criticism. Those works of literature which have

special appeal in the modern situation draw much of their
power from their use of profound religious-cultural symbols. We have in mind such symbols as Paradise, The
Flood, Sodom and Gomorrah, Belshazzar's Feast, The
End of the World. Or such figures as those of Adam, innocent or fallen; Joseph, in Egypt, that is, as Thomas Mann
presents it, in the world of the dead; Judas, an antinomian
hero, as in Robinson Jeffers; or such figures outside of
Scripture as Prometheus, Ulysses, Empedocles, the Wan-
dering Jew, Faust, or Don Juan.

The use of the above or similar myths or symbols is
illustrated by Fry's *Sleep of Prisoners* — with its evocation of the sacrifice of Isaac and other scenes of the Bible;
Sir William Walton's great musical score, *Belshazzar's
Feast;* C. F. Ramuz' apocalyptic *The End of All Men;* and
other works based on the Odyssey, the Greek tragedies,
the ancient mystery religions or some other old-world
source, fable, or archetype.

One particular example is revealing for the way in which
such ancient motifs are given wide cultural application in
our own American scene. R. W. B. Lewis has written a
volume which well illustrates how both literature and
criticism involve dimensions which are not only sociological but existential. It is entitled *The American Adam:
Innocence, Tragedy and Tradition in the Nineteenth
Century.*[13] The whole history of American literature from
James Fenimore Cooper to Faulkner is seen as presenting
the vicissitudes of Adam in a new Paradise, an Adam who
is painfully initiated into the meaning of good and evil,
and who has to come to terms not only with nature but
with history, not only with space but with time. Lewis
shows how the Adam symbol links together many of the
greatest expressions in American literature. We have in

Cooper the innocent Adam in a new unspoiled nature; in Emerson, the new Adam who is "to new-name all the beasts of the field and all the gods of the sky"; in Whitman, we have the new Adam who knows no paternity or home, but who goes forth, not to discover a world, but to create it. In Hawthorne and Henry James, we have the innocent Adam who is caught in the toils of a complex world, but whose fall brings a blessing to him, and initiation into a richer individuality. Finally we have, already forecast in Melville, the genuinely tragic Adam — the one which we meet in contemporary literature. The portrait here is of innocence and naïveté unprepared for the deeper enigmas and shocks of the human condition. A notable example of this phase of the story is exhibited to us in the book-length poem of Robert Penn Warren, *Brother to Dragons*. Here a drastic revision of the American Dream is suggested. For in the person of Thomas Jefferson, the excessive confidence of the Founding Fathers in the goodness of man and in democratic institutions meets with a stunning shock. In American literature today as inspired by the modern crisis, the greatest interest attaches to how this shock is met by a disabused and fallen Adam.

Professor Perry Miller has recently discussed this matter from a somewhat different angle in a paper entitled "The Romantic Dilemma in American Nationalism and the Concept of Nature." [14] Through all his vicissitudes the American Adam bears a unique character. He has been so stamped by his initial adventure into this new world, this virgin theater of his new civilization — by the immensities of the great plains and the forests, the limitless spaces of the West, the towering height of the mountains and the infinite coast lines — that he will always have a streak of the untamed in him, a principle of rebellion. He

will have a nostalgia for the mystery of nature and the
elemental such as appears in some of Faulkner's best
stories. Perry Miller cites the cases of figures like Thoreau,
Melville, and Whitman and traces various phases of the
dilemma in the literature and art of the last century.
Such a perspective corrects the schema presented by Lewis.
The unfallen aspect of the American Adam still survives in
a significant measure, and this fact is not to be deprecated.
The Adam of this hemisphere has had and still has a
streak of the untamed in him, a feature which theology
should not hasten to subdue. We suspect that the Almighty
takes some special pleasure in this wild strain from the
ancient stock. God must recurrently find himself bored
with such mannered peoples as the French and the Chinese. What it means, as Professor Miller points out, however, is that the American Adam will always have his
periodic revulsions against two areas of authority, highly
divergent as they are. One of these areas is that of an
elaborate civilization, especially our contemporary industrial and technical civilization. The other area is that
of institutional religion, especially in its imported forms.
Such a view throws open the possibilities of a distinctive
contribution of America to the great religious traditions.
The work of the best contemporary American writers
deserves special attention when this consideration is wid-
ened: how in them the peculiar American experience relates itself to the spiritual traditions and artistic traditions
of the West.

We have been illustrating in various ways the religious
dimensions of contemporary literature and criticism. The
objection will be raised that negation if not nihilism
dominates much of the most significant writing today.
But here we need to look closely. The conversation with

Kafka which we have cited shows how close agnosticism can come to faith. The unbelief of today is more affirmative than the shallow skepticism of yesterday. The poignant atheism of today is more pregnant than the dogmatic rationalism of yesterday. The perfect statement of the modern tragic mood is found in the words from the Gospel: "I believe; help thou mine unbelief."

Atheism in the modern artist represents a kind of purification, a transitional phase, a purification from secondhand and obsolete religious habits, a purging of inferior consolations, hopes, and sentiments. This wrestling with reality is found in unbelievers and believers. It is strikingly evident in the case of Simone Weil and her absent God. The work of this writer offers a revealing witness to the problem of grace in our time.

The German poet and critic Hans Egon Holthusen, discussing the case of the atheist poet Gottfried Benn, says some telling things on this point. He insists on the right of and the necessity for the Christian to enter with full sympathy into the nihilistic expressions of our day. Fifty years ago, he writes, we would have crossed ourselves in the presence of certain artistic tendencies. Today we must give good heed to all such seemingly alien or even blasphemous expressions. They may well carry aspects of truth that are important to the church.[15]

The fact is that both unbelievers and believers today have been lifted above a flat unimaginative and empty level of experience and thought. Both faith and atheism have become dynamic. Martin Jarrett-Kerr cites a story of Dostoievsky in which in a dream a man finds himself in another planet where there is no sin or evil, a planet, however, whose bland and insipid stagnation is disturbed and ruined by the advent of this mortal from the earth.

"The shadowy somewhat cliché-strewn picture of the
paradisal planet is shattered into reality by the coming of
the infectious but live sinful man." [16] This may serve as
a parable for the recovery in our own time of a dramatic
sense of the depths and heights of existence. The writers
identified today with negation and nihilism speak out of
this kind of experience and testify to the real dilemmas
that hide for all of us behind older sentimentalities and
illusions.

When Jean Cocteau's play *Bacchus* was produced in
Paris in 1951 it occasioned a great scandal and the author
was charged with blasphemy. The play deals with an episode of the Reformation and the representatives of the
Catholic Church are not presented in a complimentary
light. Mauriac attacked the author in the *Figaro Litéraire*,
a campaign which became notorious. Cocteau's comment
is revealing of the impatience of the modern artist with
some aspects of modern Christianity which are mawkish
and which refuse God his proper claim upon the intelli-
gence as well as upon the heart.

> Bacchus is a play about hard goodness (*la bonté dure*)
> which I oppose to soft goodness (*la bonté molle*) . . . [a
> play concerned] to give back to God the intelligence that
> is paid into the Devil's account and which was paid to him
> especially in the sixteenth century when the Devil played
> the leading part.[17]

One of the leading Christian voices of our generation,
Dietrich Bonhoeffer, martyr in a German Concentration
camp, wrote in a letter from prison in 1944:

> I often ask myself why a Christian instinct frequently
> draws me more to the religionless than to the religious,
> by which I mean not with any intention of evangelizing
> them, but rather, I might almost say, in "brotherhood." [18]

What he means is made clear in the context. The secular world has, as he says, come of age in our time of troubles. Its wrestling with the deepest questions is authentic and desperate where too often the believers, the children of light, are still out of touch with the Word of God in this generation. But this only reinforces our theme that the cleavage between the church and the arts is giving way and that a new and rewarding encounter between the two is in the making.

In this selective and fragmentary way, we have sought to open up the contemporary dialogue between religion and the arts, and to deal with the matter more particularly from the side of the arts. The preoccupation of the modern artist, as described, makes it understandable that the theologians should take a new interest in the arts. But there are other reasons for this new interest on the side of religion, and to this whole matter we will turn in our next chapter.

Chapter **II**

The Church and
the Modern Arts

Protestants often are unaware of the numinous power inherent in genuine symbols, words, acts, persons, things. They have replaced the great wealth of symbols appearing in the Christian tradition by rational concepts, moral laws, and subjective emotions.

Paul Tillich

1. Bridging the Gulf

In our first chapter, we have examined the reputed breach between Christianity and the arts and noted the signs of a new *rapprochement* between them. We then looked at the growing convergence of interest and the quickened dialogue from the side of the artist and critic. Now we propose to consider these from the side of religion. What bridges are being thrown out over the gulf from the side of the church?

Again we pause to recognize the complexity of the matter. We cannot generalize easily about the church. If our larger question is that of a new sense of responsibility on the part of Christianity toward the arts, we may well distinguish the Catholic and the Protestant aspects of the matter, but also more specialized traditions, like the Lutheran and the Calvinist. A recent American Quaker publication, by an artist who is himself a member of the Society of Friends, speaks of "their centuries of prejudice against the arts," and calls for a reform in this

respect, which, in fact, he sees as already under way.[1]
But the complexity of the matter appears in other forms.
The churches today have a quickened interest in the
ecclesiastical arts. This is a very pragmatic side of the
topic. On the other hand, many theologians are exercised
in a new way with the whole problem of aesthetics, and
the relation of beauty to holiness. Finally, many younger
churchmen identify themselves actively with the modern
movements in literature and the arts, in part because of
the light that these throw on the human situation of our
time.

Albert Schweitzer's mastery in the field of music, both
as artist and scholar, may well be mentioned here as we
introduce our whole discussion. In this respect he stands
as a symbol and augury of the reconciliation at the highest
level of religion and art, and indeed of Protestantism and
art. Barriers of suspicion against Christianity among agnostics are broken through by a man like Schweitzer, in
whom a life-affirming art corroborates a life-affirming faith.

We may also note the active participation of Karl
Barth in the recent Mozart bicentennial. Not only has the
great and austere theologian devoted a small volume to
his favorite composer, but he recently shared in the homage offered to Mozart at the University of Geneva. His
theme there was the freedom of Mozart. "He honored
Mozart, who, though Roman Catholic, and yet a Free-
mason, was utterly free of all institutional deformations,
whether ecclesiastical or political." [2]

The most obvious aspect of the churches' interest in the
arts today is their concern to purify the ecclesiastical arts.
We are aware of a veritable campaign on all sides looking
toward better church architecture, better stained glass,
better church music, better hymnals. The church in many

quarters has a bad conscience in these matters — at least we may say that some churchmen have. But this pragmatic concern drives Christians to identify norms for church arts and liturgy, and so Christians often find themselves nonplussed. Many religious traditions have not given any fundamental thought for generations to such matters.

We hear, for example, of a church committee inviting a leading architect to design a new church. The architect, who in this respect is a paragon of his profession, a Daniel come to judgment, asked the committee to provide him not only with specifications as to how the new church "plant" is to be used, but also (note!) a statement as to how the worshippers understand the ultimate meaning of the church and its worship. In the case cited, both the committee of Christian laymen and the minister himself were stricken dumb. The architect was asking the fundamental theological question. The committee knew that they wanted what they called a sanctuary, if not an auditorium, accommodation for a church school, for church dinners; they wanted a gymnasium, a study for the minister, a kitchen, rest rooms; but they did not know what a house of God was for, or what their kind of church was for. They could no doubt have answered with some clichés. But the discerning architect knew that he could not design a court of justice without some sense of the meaning of the law in our Anglo-Saxon tradition, and that he could not plan a church without some appreciation of the faith of the particular congregation in question.

Thus the problem of the ecclesiastical arts today has forced the church to examine its presuppositions about the aesthetic order. But Christians today are concerned not only with the arts in the church but with the arts generally, and this raises the same wider questions. The believer is increasingly aware of a certain provincialism here. Through a combination of circumstances the ethos of American Protestantism has often become unlovely. Rationalism has had its role in some quarters in blighting imagination and plastic expression. More generally, emphasis on the will and the moral life has had its ascetic consequences. The best-known address of John R. Mott, spoken before countless college audiences and conferences a generation ago, began with the words: "The most important aspect of religion is that which has to do with the will." But one must also say that a Main Street civilization has infected American religion with its own cultural insensitivity. It is understandable, then, that for this reason too, the churches have forfeited the support of many significant elements in our society, including many of those concerned with the arts. T. S. Eliot's earlier satire on the church, like that of John Betjemen and others today, is directed not only at its moral but also at its aesthetic obtuseness.

Betjemen's verse satirizes impartially both Anglicanism and Nonconformity. As an example, we may quote his "Calvinistic Evensong":

> The six bells stopped, and in the dark I heard
> Cold silence wait the Calvinistic word;
> For Calvin now the soft oil lamps are lit —
> Hands on their hymnals, six old women sit.
> Black-gowned and sinister, he now appears —
> Curate-in-charge of aged parish fears.
> Let, unaccompanied, that psalm begin
> Which deals most harshly with the fruits of sin!
>
> Boy! Pump the organ! Let the anthem flow
> With promise for the chosen saints below!
> Pregnant with warning the globed elm-trees wait —

Fresh coffin-wood beside the churchyard gate.
And that mauve hat three cherries decorate
Next week shall topple from its trembling perch
While wet fields reek like some long empty church.[3]

But we find another aspect of the question of religion and the arts today in the awakening interest of the theologian in the modern arts. At one level this means the discovery that art and literature are an indispensable index to the modern situation. But beyond this the theologian, recognizing the stature of much modern work and its bearing, direct or indirect, upon the problem of man today, finds himself drawn into all the issues that modern literature and art raise. And here enters the role of the believer as critic. Furthermore, when the Christian enters upon the task of a "Christian discrimination," he cannot stop with literature and the fine arts. He finds himself engaged with the problems, both aesthetic and moral, raised by the popular arts and the modern mass media.

The new interest of the churches in literature and the arts finds organized expression in various forms. At the level of the local church, we find exhibits of church architecture, expositions of religious painting and sculpture, and production of modern plays, like those of Eliot and Fry, as well as initiatives with respect to the dance and the pageant. The Riverside Church in New York has now for several years sponsored a small anthology of poetry by college writers, judges of which have included Marianne Moore, Richard Eberhart, and Mark Van Doren. Church bodies, local or regional, have also organized series of lectures or discussions bearing on the modern arts. To give two examples: a recent seminar at Drew University concerned with theology and literature attracted a good number of teachers of English. The lecturers and readers included Cleanth Brooks, Marianne Moore, and a number of theologians. Another example of such initiatives was a monthly series of lectures for pastors, under the joint auspices of Dartmouth College and the New Hampshire Congregational-Christian Churches, including lectures on Eliot, Kafka, D. H. Lawrence, Faulkner, Camus, Shaw, Graham Greene, and others, by various scholars. Of special significance is the work today in theological seminaries, of which we shall speak later.

The most striking organized activity in this field, however, has been that connected with the Department of Worship and the Arts of the National Council of Churches.[4] This department has organized separate commissions for drama, art, architecture, music, and literature. Each commission is made up of both artists and churchmen, laymen and clergy, and each has undertaken special tasks appropriate to its field. Thus the Commission on the Drama, which includes Norris Houghton, Francis Fergusson, and John Mason Brown, has been represented at the international Conference on Religious Drama at Oxford, and proposes among other things to encourage the writing and production of new plays "which reflect the religious concerns of contemporary Christians."

A three-year program in religious drama was initiated recently in Union Theological Seminary with the help of the Rockefeller Foundation. In its first year it was directed by E. Martin Browne, who had rendered distinguished service with the British Drama League and the Religious Drama Society of Great Britain. His role in the production of plays at Canterbury Cathedral like T. S. Eliot's *Murder in the Cathedral* and Fry's *A Sleep of Prisoners* will be recalled. One of the first plays produced at Union Theological Seminary under the auspices of the program was a dramatic version of Melville's *Billy Budd,* a play which is rapidly entering the repertoire of groups in churches and seminaries as well as in colleges and universities.

The Commission on Architecture, which includes leading architects and the editors of the leading architectural journals in this country, held a recent session in Indianapolis in conjunction with the annual meeting of the American Institute of Architects, meeting in a church designed by Saarinen, and hearing a paper on church architecture by Pietro Belluschi. This commission is faced with the formidable task of correcting the sterile and derivative style in which thousands of churches are built in this country each year.

The Commission on Literature has included W. H. Auden, Cleanth Brooks, the editors of the *Yale* and *Sewanee* reviews, the novelist Frederick Buechner, and others. This group has been involved in planning conferences, and in working out bibliographies on theology and literature and the basic issues of literary criticism.

Perhaps the best single example of how far joint discussion of aesthetic questions has gone today is the symposium entitled *Spiritual Problems in Contemporary Literature,* edited by Stanley R. Hopper, under the auspices of the Institute for Religious and Social Studies.[5] This volume, dedicated to Theodore Spencer, contains eighteen papers under three heads: Religion and the Artist's Situation; Religion and the Artist's Means; Religion and the Artist's Beliefs. Contributors include J. J. Sweeney, Theodore Spencer, Delmore Schwartz, David Daiches, William Barrett, Denis de Rougemont, Wallace Fowlie, and Kenneth Burke, as well as a number of theologians.

2. Victorian Idealism and Symbolic Realism

With this preliminary survey before us we turn to our
main consideration in this chapter. What are the deeper
factors in the new concern of the churches with the arts,
and with the modern arts? How is this new interest being
expressed? In what way is the church making amends for
its shortcomings in this area?

In many quarters we find among Christians today a new
grasp of the whole problem of symbolic expression. Even
those churches which we call liturgical, and which have
maintained a positive attitude toward the arts, now recognize a new dimension in this area. The student of religion
has learned to assign more significance to myth, ritual,
and art in the understanding of the world's faiths. Psychology and anthropology have contributed their insights
to the matter.

Thus the perceptive theologian today sees the arts not
merely as embellishments of worship or strategies for
religious propaganda. Nor is he satisfied to set the arts
over against daily life as an inspirational resource, and to
say that religion must use the resources of the Spirit —
meaning Beauty, Poetry, and Imagination — as compensations for the prosaic and utilitarian world in which
modern men live. Here again we have the idealistic fallacy
of which we have spoken. Such a dichotomy of prose and
poetry, of actuality and dreams, or of realism and imagination, is really an escape philosophy. It disparages art and
worship as mere consolations, and in effect abandons the
actual life of men as unredeemable. It capitulates to the
banishment of the arts and of worship from a materialist
world, from a rational-technological age.

The theologian today recognizes that even the materialist lives not by creature comforts, prosperity, and success, but by his own symbols and images, his own myths and rituals. The conflict today is not between matter and spirit, but between two kinds of spirit; not between prose and imagination, but between a true and false imagination; not even, finally, between ugliness and beauty, because "beauty" has ever to be redefined, and because what some would call beauty and ideality cannot save. Cocteau's pungent dictum was that the artist "must always keep running faster than beauty." The case is the same as with morality. As soon as the conceptions of beauty and virtue become fixed they are no longer beautiful or moral.

The churchman today is recognizing that the arts are more than embellishment, more than inspirational and mood-creating. They convey more than emotion; they convey knowledge. They convey more than a mood; they convey meaning. Different art forms communicate different meanings. Our ultimate fealties are tied up with this or that representation. What finally is important is the symbol and the kind of symbol, the imagery and the kind of imagery, the myth and the kind of myth. For symbols convey truth or error. They mediate illusion or reality. Sentimental symbols of aspiration, dreams, and ideality may effect temporary reflexes of beatitude or induce charmed states of euphoria, but this is escapism. This is religious romanticism. There was a time, it is true, when Christian transcendentalism like Christian Platonism incorporated a substantial core of the Christian view of man and evil, so as to constitute valid versions of Christian theology. But these strains of Christian idealism have been attenuated and washed out.

The best theology today, in its repudiation of a rhetorical religious idealism, finds itself in agreement with a re-

current note in contemporary poetry: Hebraic concrete-
ness is more at home with modern verse than Greek
Platonism. T. S. Eliot said of Henry James that he had "a
mind so fine, no idea [no ideal!] could violate it." The
poets at least ask, with Marianne Moore, for "real toads
in imaginary gardens." The theme which runs through
the glorious celebration of the imagination in Wallace
Stevens is similar:

> We keep coming back and coming back
> To the real: to the hotel instead of the hymns
> That fall upon it out of the wind. . . .
>   We seek
> Nothing beyond reality. Within it,
> Everything, the spirit's alchemicana. . . .
>
>   Not grim
> Reality, but reality grimly seen.[6]

These things are said everywhere in Stevens. The "fes-
tival sphere" of the imagination, he says, begins from the
"crude collops." [7]

The poet Richard Wilbur recurs to a similar theme.
Take, for example, his poem "A World Without Objects
is a Sensible Emptiness." The poem describes the alluring
but accursed mirages of the mystic and the idealist. The
poet is advised to turn back from the "long empty oven"
of the desert to the real world and its homely objects:
here is

> . . . The spirit's right
> Oasis, light incarnate.[8]

One may illustrate the new maturity in religious attitudes to the arts by noticing what has gone on in the
theological seminaries in recent years. In times past theological training was concerned, as indeed it always should

be, with the professional and ecclesiastical aspects of the arts. The future minister was given some introduction to church music and hymnody, though even here he was often later at the mercy of his director of music. Some real effort was made in many seminaries to further his acquaintance with literature. This represented a dim carryover of the ancient claims of rhetoric on the preacher. And, indeed, the preacher should be, in the ancient sense, a grammarian, at home in letters, languages, eloquence, and the classics. Both for his own spiritual culture and for the enrichment of preaching, courses were offered in English poetry as in the world's classics of devotion.

Many ministers today remember with appreciation certain teachers in whose seminary classes Homer and Moses were both read, the Sybil testified as well as David, and the springs of Helicon were sought as well as those of Jordan. One may single out the names of Willard L. Sperry at Harvard, who shared with his students his lifelong devotion to Wordsworth, Charles A. Dinsmore of Yale, with his contagious enthusiasm for Dante, Lynn Harold Hough at Drew, Earl Marlatt at Boston University, and Fred Eastman of the Chicago Theological Seminary. If we go farther back, we find A. H. Strong, whose books, including *The Great Poets and Their Theology,* rested on years of seminary teaching in the Rochester Theological Seminary. Such teachers were chiefly concerned with the Christian poets. In England, similar examples were to found in Stopford Brooke's *Theology in the English Poets* and in the volumes on the spiritual resources in Browning and in Francis Thompson by Robert A. Hutton.

The new interest in the arts in the seminaries and among theologians contrasts sharply with the approaches mentioned. It is no longer only a question of the Sacred Lyre and of the cultural formation of the clergy. More urgent today is the whole question of imaginative vehicles, of symbolization in religion. The basic semantic question in religious discourse is raised, and the whole problem of communication. Almost every department of theological study is involved at this level, and this means attention not only to the symbols and images of the Christian faith; it also means attention to the symbols and images and art forms of the contemporary world as they are encountered not only in literature and the fine arts, but also and not least in the mass media.

We realize better today that society lives by its myths, its favorite symbols, and these are not idle or interchangeable. The Cross is one thing, and the Swastika is another. The Sheaf of Wheat is one thing, and the Fascus is another. The "Battle Hymn of the Republic" speaks one faith and the "Internationale" another. The Lincoln Memorial and the tomb of Lenin evoke and nourish mutually exclusive images of mankind.

Society lives by its symbols, and society represents a battleground of competing symbols; sometimes a battle to the death, sometimes a devitalizing stalemate within a family or nation of incompatible loyalties and banners: in France, the Revolution over against Catholic order; in our Southern states, ancient nostalgias over against a genuine agrarian humanism — each with their evocative emblems.

Social responsibility and discernment require a clear perception of such rival myths and their power, recognition of such competing visions and rituals, ability to exorcise those that are malign, and to reconcile those that are benign. Society lives by its images; hence its life is stagnant and moribund where the living images fail. In any case, the church must recognize the situation. It is more important to discern the actual operative myths of civilization than the formal clichés of its political orators. A democratic society may proclaim its democratic dogmas, but the same society may be governed by undemocratic nostalgias and passions fed by obsolete dreams. The church itself may proclaim its Christian principles, but Christians may be ruled by sub-Christian images.

Archibald MacLeish well states the importance of the myths of an age, what happens when they fade, and the responsibility of the poet, and, we may add, the believer, in renewing them.

> A world ends when its metaphor has died.
> An age becomes an age, all else beside,
> When sensuous poets in their pride invent
> Emblems for the soul's consent
> That speak the meanings men will never know
> But man-imagined images can show:
> It perishes when those images, though seen,
> No longer mean. . . .[9]

W. II. Auden, in his Harvard Phi Beta Kappa poem in 1946, "Under Which Lyre," [10] provides us with a pungent portrayal of the running battle that goes on on any campus between two ancient symbols and their respective following: Apollo vs. Hermes.

The main point is that when we say art, we say image; and when we say image or symbol, we say meaning, we say communication. The arts, old and new, the fine arts, the practical arts, and the popular arts are peculiarly the carriers of meaning and value in our society as in all societies. The church is learning that it cannot ignore such expressions of the society in which it lives. The en-

counter of the Gospel with the world, whether in evangel-
ism, religious education, apologetics, or theology, requires
a deep appreciation of, and initiation into, the varied
symbolic expressions of culture. It is not enough for the
church to take account of what the social sciences tell us
about the communities in which it works. It is rather
through such sensitive recorders as poet, dramatist, novelist, and painter that we are enabled to go below the
surface in assessing our time and thus take full cognizance
of the fateful and intangible factors which operate in the
hearts of men.

Not the least of the contributions of artist and poet have
been their profound portrayals of the human situation in
our period. We have here a double resource. On the one
hand, the arts can be taken as documents which mirror
the time — and here we can call on all symbolic expression, from the purest and most sophisticated productions
to the cinema, radio, and television. But in the most
responsible forms of contemporary art we have further a
powerful criticism of our age. The great banes of modern
life are exposed and scrutinized. One has only to call to
mind the growing library of modern classics, from Kafka
and Joyce to Auden and Faulkner, to recognize that we
would never have reached so penetrating a criticism of
the modern crisis if we had had to depend on the preacher
or the theologian or the social scientist.

More striking still is the far-reaching body of critical
interpretation and annotation, which has grown up about
the work of the modern poets and artists. This work is
indeed first of all directed to aesthetic assessment; but
modern works like D. H. Lawrence's *The Plumed Serpent,*
T. S. Eliot's *The Family Reunion,* Auden's *Age of
Anxiety,* Silone's *Bread and Wine,* and Camus' *The*

Plague, along with various works of Henry James, Thomas Mann, Malraux, and Sartre — all such works call for a kind of criticism which transcends a narrow aestheticism. Questions of strictly literary morphology and antecedent widen out into the most fundamental moral-cultural observation. To read the best critical work of writers like Eliot, Matthiessen, Tate, Trilling, Warren, and many others, is to find oneself sooner or later in the midst of a far more searching debate on moral and theological questions than is found in much of the religious literature of our time. The critics are in some respects better educated than the theologians — they know their modern sciences as well as their humanities, and they are working upon contemporary classics which uncover the existential situation of men today and the moral factors which play upon it.

The theologian today has discovered the wider contribution that the arts can make to his own task. He has also brought Christian insights to the interpretation of the arts. In reading contemporary criticism, one is frequently struck with one limitation of the secular critics. They often lack the kind of discriminating understanding of figures like Augustine, Aquinas, Luther, and Calvin, or of the different strains of Catholic and Puritan piety, which is required for an adequate assessment of a great deal of English literature. Professor John E. Smith of Yale, in discussing recent work on the metaphysical poets, has called attention to such weaknesses as well as to the continuing misunderstanding of the Puritan "mistrust of the senses," its motivation and its limits. There is an obligation on the critic, as Smith says, "to be as sound and critical in theology as in aesthetics." [11]

We return to the situation in the theological seminaries

today, for it is an indication of the wider interest of the church in the arts generally. In many such graduate schools of religion courses are regularly offered dealing not only with the ecclesiastical arts but with theology and the arts, with religion and culture, with the modern poets and novelists. The primary concern is with those works in literature or the graphic arts which testify to the deeper movements in the modern world, disclose the conflict of loyalties in the modern soul, or dramatize the vicissitudes of the Christian tradition in the modern world. Associated with this search, however, is the impulse to recapture for the Christian faith a proper role in the assessment of the arts ancient and modern.

The question may legitimately be raised why the theological seminary should offer instruction in literature and the arts, rather than send its students to the appropriate departments. It is not a question, however, of one or the other. The seminary or department of religion presupposes the work done, for example, in the English department. For graduate degrees, joint supervision is indicated for such interdisciplinary programs. On the other hand, the context in which such studies are carried out differs as between a given department of the humanities and a school of religion. In the latter, it is ordinarily possible to relate a given work of art or literature to a wide variety of religious considerations more fully than is the case in the college classroom. The ultimate canons of literary criticism arise from the literary disciplines. But these disciplines themselves have been known to profit by what could first appear as nonaesthetic considerations. Literature and the arts have such universal significance that they represent public domain; and it is not surprising that the same classics, ancient and modern, turn up not only in departments of English, but in departments of philosophy, or religion, or even of social science. The case is a little like that of psychology today. The seminaries have extensive work in religion and psychology, and theologians deal with this field in such a way as to contribute at least suggestive footnotes to the domain of the psychologist and the psychiatrist.

3. The Scandal of the Modern Arts

The new more serious concern of theologians with the arts today dates, as we have suggested, from their recognition that the modern arts are of first importance for assessment of the modern situation. Thus we may take note of how three representative theologians, one Russian Orthodox, one Protestant, and one Roman Catholic, have appealed, in their writings, to modern art in their exploration of modern man. Nicholas Berdyaev, in his book *The End of Our Time*,[12] documents the dissolution of the humanist epoch by referring to modern painting. What he calls the dismemberment of man in post-impressionist painting, the fragmentation of the human form and of the coherent field of objective perception, is taken as a symptom and an intuitive recognition of the modern situation. These features of modern art, with their parallels in literature, signify the approach of our world to a more profound phase or epoch — a new Middle Age — in which society would live in more direct relation to its creative ground. Post-impressionism and surrealism indicate a deeper vision and a deeper wisdom than were possible in either the humanism of the Enlightenment or that of mediaeval scholasticism.

Again, in a Protestant work, Paul Tillich's *The Religious Situation*,[13] we find a theologian using modern painting and art with striking cogency as evidences of a changing cultural and religious situation. Here the point is made that changes in the arts anticipate social change. The shift in the arts toward expressionism and abstraction is taken not as a sign of decadence but as evidence of a new depth of experience and of religious dimension. Tillich's concern with the arts has found ever-new expression in his later writings and teaching. The topic arises for him both in connection with his interest in the religious grounds of culture and in his interest in symbolism. It was inevitable that these concerns should have led him to his more recent forcible statements about religious art, his condemnation of religious *kitsch*, and his forthright defense of modern art in its aspects of distortion, nonrepresentationalism, and abstraction. Tillich has also maintained that the church today should have a vanguard of men and women qualified to interpret the significance of contemporary art for the believer, and able to make contact with the influential movements of our time in art, literature, and criticism.

On the side of Catholic theology, we find our example in Jacques Maritain. His witness to the religious significance of the modern artist is all the more welcome, because the common tendency of Roman Catholic and Anglo-Catholic cultural critics is to disparage modern art and poetry as decadent and demoralizing. Maritain, like our American critic Wallace Fowlie, can deal favorably with Rimbaud and Baudelaire and the whole creative line of those French poets who are often disparaged as *les poètes maudits*. In a series of writings which recently culminated in his *Creative Intuition in Art and Poetry*,[14] Maritain studies the new exploration of consciousness offered to us in modern works and finds a new intuitive self-revelation of man as well as a widening of the resources of the artist. Granted that the dissolution of the older patterns of belief and order is reflected in modern works, this very situation, with the anguish consequent upon it, has made possible a richer sensibility in the artist, and a more profound metaphysical awareness. The initiation into tragedy and evil made possible a break with earlier romanticism, and the imagination found itself again at grips with a total human nature and experience. The arts were emancipated from their traditional imprisonment in subjectivity and sentiment. This influence spread to have its effect upon Joyce, Pound, and Eliot. Here, as we know, the liberation of English poetry was furthered by an appeal back of the nineteenth century, to Old English, Elizabethan, and seventeenth-century models.

The controversy that continues with ever-renewed virulence over the question of modern art, both among the experts and in the general public, is of more than aesthetic importance. This controversial situation involves the churches directly. It is always interesting to note the bitterness of feeling which is aroused in disputes over exhibitions of modern painting or with respect to the award of some national prize to a modern poet. This polemic violence is an indication that men's basic securities are held to be at stake, their values, their way of life. We have here transparent evidence that the arts are finally fateful and that men obscurely recognize it.

An increasing number of theologians are taking sides with the modernist movement in the arts, but the mass of churchmen are unacquainted with such movements and scandalized by them. The traditional-minded Christian,

like the average citizen, finds modern art "difficult," but
he is especially indisposed to its appreciation by what we
have called the idealistic fallacy and moralistic attitudes.
The traditionalist is often unable to distinguish between
significant modern works and those merely faddist or
immature modern experiments which rightly arouse his
suspicion. Churchmen can also easily be persuaded that
modern art has subversive political or economic implications. The established citizen always has some suspicion
of the artist, the Bohemian. He is uncomfortable in the
presence of groups that maintain so intransigent a way of
life, and which treat so lightly his own axioms of security
and respectability. This is all the more true in a period of
cultural disarray and of incipient hysteria, when the artist
and writer appear to be disaffected with respect to prevailing codes, and addicted to what appears to be immoral-
ism or even blasphemy.

In the light of this situation, one of the most interesting
current functions of the theologian is to interpret to the
church as a whole the true significance of the modern arts.
It is a minor aspect of the task to insist that art should
not necessarily be viewed as only a pleasurable and indul-
gent matter. As Ernst Cassirer has said,

> The beauty of the work of art is never "easy." The enjoy-
> ment of art does not originate in a softening or relaxing
> process, but in the intensification of all our energies. . . .
> Art demands the fullest concentration.[15]

More drastic for the traditionalist is the demand made
by the arts upon men for the revision of their outlook.
The text for this may be found in two lines of a poem by
Rilke, his "Archaic Torso of an Apollo":

> These is no part of it that does not see you,
> You must change your life.[16]

For modern art, modern poetry, at their best say to men: You must change your life! Such art represents a demand, even a rebuke. It sees through us. Much of the scandal of such work lies in its implicit deflation of generally accepted ideals, and not only aesthetic ideals. Works like those of Joyce, Eliot, and Faulkner come as a shock. They reflect an unromantic, even a harsh, conception of life. There is an interesting analogy between the surgical acerbity of much modern art and the inexorable sobriety of neo-orthodox theology. In any case, the modern writer challenges men to revise their mood and attitude. He says that cherished decorums are misconceived, and that cherished securities are not enough. That which is made so much of as "health" and "sanity" in accepted attitudes is incriminated as sickness. Thus the implicit injunction of the modern work of art: You must change your life!

It is this feature of modern art which makes men blind with rage. It is like disparaging a man's mother country. The best modern art exposes people. This explains the irrational violence of their reactions. Any notable recognition of the new arts occasions a kind of panic in those of the established order. They have a bitterly aggrieved sense of desertion. They are like children who think the circus procession is coming their way — and suddenly find, to their disappointment, that it is going down another street.

The appreciation of the modern arts in certain church circles is therefore one of the most important features of the whole situation. It is one aspect of the awakening of the churches generally to a better knowledge of the world about them. It is indispensable to the purification of the sacred arts. More important still, it will contribute to a new theological seriousness, a greater discrimination in the matter of Christian symbols. In some periods, Christians need to be awakened from their dogmatic slumber, for, as the letter kills, dogmatism destroys sensibility. But today, it is widely true that the churches need to be awakened from their undogmatic slumber: [17] they have lost awareness of the fateful issues of good and evil, of salvation and damnation. This kind of salutary shock is provided by the modern arts: not only by Christian, but by agnostic artists and writers.

Thus the church is discovering the modern arts in two respects: it is learning to diagnose the age through their insights, and it is being exposed to what the modern arts can teach it, what they have to say about its own chief concerns.

Chapter III

Theology and
Aesthetic Judgment

It almost looks today as though the Church
alone offers any prospect for the recovery of
the sphere of freedom (art, education, friend-
ship and play, "aesthetic existence," as Kierkegaard called it).
> Dietrich Bonhoeffer, in a letter
> from prison of January 23, 1944

If the church is awakening today to a new sense of responsibility with regard to the arts, whether sacred or secular, it is very important that Christians should be clear about their basic aesthetics: their understanding of the nature of art, the criteria of good and bad art and good and bad poetry, and the meaning of symbols. This is even more important if believers wish to further the current *rapprochement* between Christianity and the arts. Any profitable conversation between the theologian and the artist or critic requires at least some degree of sophistication on both sides.

As with the general population, Christians often not only lack taste and the canons of taste, but they hold superannuated ideas of the meaning of beauty, ideas which are both theologically and aesthetically defective. The art and architecture associated with one of our leading denominations, which shall be nameless, in a region which shall be nameless, is characterized by one leading citizen of that region as "among the ugliest things in modern civilization — unspeakable." Yet Christians with

63

these kinds of handicaps have felt themselves fully qualified
to embark on programs for the censorship of modern art
and literature.

The confusions of the contemporary scene are well illustrated when we put alongside of each other on the one
hand the banning of modern classics by good Christian
people, and on the other hand Julian Green's denuncia-
tion of the pernicious influence of the painter Raphael on
religious art. Green writes:

> In an evil hour for Christianity this magnificent genius
> [Raphael] stereotyped all the incidents of the life of Christ.
> . . . but Raphael did much more, he infected and saturated
> the minds of millions with dull commonplaces about the
> Gospels. . . . he crowded the invisible with chromos. . . .
> Raphael is probably one of the most dangerous heretics
> since the church began; his heresy is a subtle one which
> begins with a yawn and ends in nausea.[1]

One of the reassuring features of the current deepen-
ing of religion is the new concern with what has been
called "Christian discrimination." Certain elements in
the church feel an obligation to come to terms vigorously
with modern culture and its various expressions on the
basis of sound theological norms. Such Christian assessment is directed for one thing toward the popular arts
of the time, whether moving picture, radio, television,
and comic strip or the best-seller novel and the Broadway
success. Judgment in such matters need not be always
disapproving. A great deal of the make-believe, entertain-
ment, and even escape in such art forms is both talented
and innocent; but distinctions must be drawn between the
genuine and the specious, between works which relate
themselves to reality and those which falsify it. And if
the real nature of things can be falsified by a crass sensa-

tionalism of sex and violence, it can also be falsified by
pseudo-idealism and sentimentality. Many supposedly in-
nocuous popular novels and plays are far more toxic and
censorable than the so-called pornographic paperbacks or
the lowly comic strip.

But a more interesting aspect of Christian discrimination appears in its application to the fine arts and its participation in high-level literary criticism. Such assessment
of the arts will of course share common ground with the
best secular criticism. We shall discuss later the question
whether there can really be such a thing as an autonomous
Christian criticism or Christian aesthetic and shall decide
against it. But let us note how large a place is occupied in
contemporary literary criticism by the problem of literature and belief. The theological critic who is free from
any apologetic motivation may often be specially qualified
to contribute to this discussion. It is evident in any case
that a number of the major writers of our time are
themselves Christian. For the interpretation of their work
the critic with an inside knowledge of the history of Christian theology and Christian art has certain special resources.

A wider consideration bearing on the validity of a
Christian role in criticism today is the whole situation
of the arts and their interpretation. The modern crisis
has set a question mark against all the great systems of
aesthetics. Both classicist and romantic textbooks in this
field are today discounted. The standing views of literature
and the arts have long been determined by what we can
call classical humanism or some modern version of it.
This whole humanistic conception is based on a view of
man which goes back to Greece. We recognize today,
however, how different the Hellenic view or views of

man were from the biblical. The understanding of man in the New Testament, the psychology and indeed the sociology implicit there, are radically different from that of the classical world. It follows that any corollaries for the aesthetic order will be correspondingly different. These distinctions have been blurred in Western philosophy and aesthetics.

The classical tools and canons for the assessment of literature are increasingly inadequate. The theologian Bonhoeffer notes that old classical or romantic shibboleths are no longer useful: "It is all too easy for us," he writes, "to acquiesce in Nietzsche's crude alternatives of 'Apolline' and 'Dionysian,' or, as we would say, demonic beauty. Nothing could be farther from the truth. Take for example Brueghel or Velasquez . . . or the French impressionists. Here we have a beauty which is neither classical nor demonic but is simply earthly though it has its own proper place." [2] Now it was precisely the "earthly" realistic note which Christianity introduced into Western literature. Man is treated empirically, as creature among creatures, in his psychosomatic unity. He is defined by his heart not by his spirit. His fate is defined by history and not by a changeless order of ideas or of being.

The rejection of the older aesthetic axioms and categories is evidenced in the best contemporary literature as it is in modern works on criticism. A modern poet like William Carlos Williams is not interested in such categories as Dionysiac or Apollonian, or in such ideals as that of the sublime, or the rhetorical, or what is called "classic perfection." Even the categories of tragedy and comedy are looked at askance. The category of tragedy is hard to work with today either as a dramatic form or as a critical tool. "Tragedy" and "comedy" in the humanist tradition are insufficiently *serious*. Thus Wallace Stevens in his ever-renewed meditation on the real keeps coming back to his insistence that it is the very humble actual given in the world of experience which is the *sine qua non* of the imagination. True seriousness, he says, lies neither in tragedy nor comedy but in the everyday and the ordinary:

> The serious reflection is composed
> Neither of comic nor tragic but of commonplace.[3]

But it is especially Erich Auerbach, in his book *Mimesis*,[4] who demonstrates the earthly and humble note which Christianity has introduced and kept alive in Western literature. This book of Auerbach's breaks new ground. For here we have a professional scholar in comparative literature who shows the continuing revolution effected in the literature of the West by the Hebraic-Christian influence. He uses passages from the writings of the Bible to set off by contrast the special virtues and limitations of the classics, and pursues the implications of this contrast through mediaeval and modern literature. He everywhere insists upon the inseparable relation of the formal features in the writings in question with the underlying doctrine of man. The insights of a book of this kind suggest the contribution that a theologically oriented criticism can make today.

As the subtitle of Auerbach's book indicates, he is interested in distinguishing different kinds of realism. The realism of the Greek epics consists in their exhaustive detail of presentation, the full spacial and temporal evocation, the vivid immediacy of unilinear surface portrayal. The realism of the biblical narratives — for examples, the sacrifice of Isaac and the denial of Christ by Peter —

is one that foregoes any such wealth of detail or such
seamless continuities. The import lies not in the delighted
enjoyment of full sensuous delineation but in the background evoked, the depth of reality (*Wirklichkeitsfülle
und Lebenstiefe*). No doubt there are generic overtones
in each of the two types. But the biblical episodes, drawn
from a wholly different world of forms, involve us as readers at a moral or moral-existential level which is quite
different from the way in which, say, the farewell of Hec-
tor involves our common human nature. Thus Friedrich
Gogarten can say of the biblical accounts that not only
are they "histories," but in them history itself — and our
history — takes place. Auerbach can therefore observe
that Abraham, Jacob, and Moses are more real to us than
the Homeric figures, not because they are presented in
more tangible and sensuous immediacy — quite the contrary — but because the problematic bewildering aspects
of life as we know them are present in the former. We
are reminded of the remark of Jaques Rivière about the
characters in the novels of Stendhal, that they are individuals not creatures, and that "in them humanity is without
its wound." Stendhal's characters are "nothing but the
sum of their passions."

A second and related theme made much of by Auerbach and also one significant for a Christian role in criticism today has to do with the nonaristocratic level of the
biblical narrative and dramatis personae. The point is
only in part that pagan literature prefers those of high
rank for its protagonists except in certain genres like
comedy and idyl. More important is the fact that pagan
literature — note the illustrations from Petronius, Taci-
tus, and so on — offers only a static view of political
processes. Social forces arising from the obscure milieus of

slaves, soldiers, artisans attract no genuine curiosity or imaginative reflection. The inner processes of history are thus overlooked.

Moreover, in late paganism a certain fixed idea of high style became established (with long antecedents of *Stiltrennung* in the Greek writers), which served as a barrier to genuine realism and to ordinary scenes and subject matter. The contrast with the biblical naïveté and earthiness appears here. In the Old Testament

> the sublime working of God reaches so deeply into everyday experience that the two domains of the sublime and the everyday are not only not in fact separated but are fundamentally inseparable.[5]

Passing to the New Testament, such a narrative as that of Peter's denial of Christ falls into the class of a *fait divers* or insignificant police court episode. Yet this *fait divers* is heavy with world-historical and cosmic overtones. It is understandable then that the biblical experience and writings

> begat a new high style, one which in no way scorned the commonplace and one which took up into itself the sensuous realistic, yes the hated and despised low order of the *sarks*.[6]

To put it in another way, that kind of subject matter which has been proper only to the low style of comedy and satire was now dealt with in terms of the sublime and the eternal.

Considerations of this kind bear on literary work and its criticism today. The humanistic tradition is always in danger of reverting to the limitations of classic literature — offering us individuals and not creatures, and humanity without its wound. The realism of the more notable contemporary influences — Proust, Joyce, Virginia Woolf, Thomas Mann, Gide — is close to and indebted to the biblical realism, as Gogarten has shown.[7]

However, when a theologian ventures into the exacting field of literary criticism he runs into many dangers. In the contemporary conversation between religion and the arts there is no responsibility of the churchman which is more important or delicate. We have noted the demand upon the secular critic that he be as sound and discriminating in theology as in aesthetics. The converse is true. The theologian engaged in the interpretation of literature must be as sound and as discriminating in aesthetics as in theology. Literary criticism has become a highly sophisticated activity. At no point has it reached more general agreement than in rejecting a dogmatic approach to works of the imagination.

1. "What has Athens to do with Jerusalem?"

When we try to come closer to what is involved in any definition of a Christian discrimination in the arts or a Christian aesthetic, we are met by a radical difficulty. There is a basic anomaly in the relation of the Gospel to human culture that it both condemns it and nourishes it. The church both denies civilization and creates it. In the Scriptures and in the early church the negative aspects appear most often. As Tertullian wrote: "What has Athens to do with Jerusalem?" The New Testament offers us several classic utterances bearing on this iconoclasm. When the disciples point out to Christ the magnificence of the temple of Herod his stern reply announcing its utter destruction appears to disparage all such considerations.

The Greek word *kalos,* in the sense of beautiful, appears only once or twice on the lips of Jesus in the Gospels, most clearly with reference to a beautiful deed — that of the anointing at Bethany. Yet it would be mistaken to generalize Jesus' words about the fate of the temple. We know that he could recognize the beauty in natural objects — the lilies of the field. For Jesus as for prophet and psalmist the aesthetic order merges with the religious but is not absent. In his words we find the attribute of glory ascribed not only to heaven but to the earth, and to the doomed city of Jerusalem itself in the words:

> Do not swear at all, even by heaven, for it is the throne of God, or by the earth, for it is his footstool, or by Jerusalem, for it is the city of the great King.

In the letters of Paul we find the same paradox. Just as the wisdom of man is folly with God so the eloquence and the rhetoric of the world would empty the Gospel of its power. Christianity attacks human life at so deep a level that it disallows all existing culture. How can one define the Christian aesthetic in these conditions? Here again we find the paradox. Just as Paul immediately checks himself and insists that the Gospel does represent a kind of wisdom, so he can affirm that it uses its own kind of words or language or rhetoric, taught by the Spirit. And he can write:

> Whatever is lovely, whatever is gracious, if there is any excellence . . . think about these things.

Thus for Paul there is a bridge between Jerusalem and Athens. Yet

Chrysostom points out how naïve the Christian is if he
proposes to prove at any price that Paul was accomplished.
No, he should acknowledge gladly that he was unpolished.
Only so do we recognize how great a miracle it is that in
spite of all he overcame Plato and his pupils — a miracle
only explainable in terms of the grace of God.[8]

It is always interesting to see how the true classicists
deal with Paul. They must see him as a barbarian, yet
they have to find phrases to credit him with some sort of
eloquence. Nothing illustrates better the humanistic prejudice or the inadequacy of the classic aesthetic categories.
H. J. C. Grierson has called St. Paul the next great romantic after Plato. This is a meaningless concession.
Gilbert Murray can speak of him as "one of the great
names in Greek literature." Wilamowitz-Moellendorff is
more illuminating. For him Paul is "a classic of Hellen-
ism." We cite R. H. Strachan's summary:

> Paul's Christian faith, compelled to utter itself in the
> Greek language, created a new style at a period when style
> had become manner. His Greek models itself on no school
> . . . yet his Greek remains Greek, and his vocabulary and
> style are comparatively little Hebraized — a contrast with
> the Gospels. The reason is, says Moellendorff, that Paul's
> thinking . . . comes direct from the heart, "spontaneously
> in a precipitated gushing stream . . . at last someone speaks
> in Greek out of a fresh inward experience in life . . . to
> him all literature is a bauble; he is without any artistic
> vein. All the greater is the estimate we must form of the
> artistic effects which he yet achieves." [9]

It is evident that this statement of Moellendorff begs the
question as to what is "artistic," or at least uses this category in a very limited context.

The fact is that Paul's letters reflect the double aspect

of the rise of the Christian religion: on the one hand the eschatological judgment of the world and its forms and structures, especially of the ancient world and its views of man and culture; and on the other hand the deeper ground of what we can call the order of creation or general revelation. Any sharing by Christians in aesthetic discussion must take account of both these primordial aspects.

If we turn to the Gospels we note that this literary genre has no precedent in Greek or any other literature. Of course we may if we wish exclude them from any enquiry into aesthetics or rhetoric by assigning them to a special sacred category of revelation. But this is in effect to deny the Incarnation. Or we can pretend that the Gospels fall into a familiar category such as that of tragedy or biography. This is in effect the approach of those who read the Bible "as literature." The Bible is indeed literature but not of a kind that can be forced into our usual Western categories. So much the worse for the academic categories. Our bondage to Greek aesthetics must be overcome, just as in analogous ways we have been delivered from Western provinciality by the study of Chinese art and literature.

The relation of the Gospel to art is illuminated by the attitudes of the church in the early centuries. The early Christians, as it were, fasted from art as commonly understood. So Wladimir Weidlé can say that early Christian art was in fact no art at all. It was "a mortification of art." The wall paintings of the catacombs were signs rather than symbols.[10] Yet, as Father Georges Florovsky points out, these inartistic signs were yet real symbols if seen in a scriptural context. Again it is a question of whether we use the term "art" in a narrow, canonical sense or not.

The early Church Fathers represent a similar absti-
nence from secular literary practice.[11] Irenaeus writes:

> You will not look for the art of words among us who live
> among the Celts and speak mainly the Barbarian languages.
> We have not learned it; nor the power of representation;
> we have not practiced it.

Origen explains that "if the disciples had used the arts
of Greek rhetoric, it would have appeared as if Jesus was
the founder of a new philosophy." What is most interesting in the case of Origen is that like some other Fathers
he hesitated about writing at all. He notes the superiority
of oral instruction, face to face with his pupils and con-
gregations. The Gospel as the Word of God is properly
spoken to the ear and not written for the eye. Yet he justifies the necessity of writing, if done with pure motives, for
the purposes of wider persuasion. The Church Fathers,
says Franz Overbeck, "are writers who do not want to be
such." Nevertheless, Augustine formally defended the
idea of a Christian *rhetor* and argued that the writers of
Scripture had combined wisdom and skill in the loftiest
measure.

We cannot here survey the whole story of Christian attitudes toward art. The theologian today who seeks a basis
for Christian discrimination can learn much from the
oscillations of attitude and the special causes for each.

2. Romantic Views of the King James Version

We have spoken of the basic anomaly with reference to
Christianity and the arts which appears in the New Testament depreciation of culture. No Christian approach to

the arts can ever overlook this. The Bible, its literary forms, and its view of nature and inspiration will always be a primary consideration in any modern Christian philosophy of art. If we may be allowed a brief excursus at this point, we would like to raise some questions about the attitude of many Christians today toward the King James Version of Scripture. The entirely justifiable appreciation of the Authorized Version — or what was actually the third authorized version — of the Bible often conceals a romantic and inadequate version of Christianity.

We have in mind those groups, which include many intellectuals, who fail to see beyond the literary prestige of this version, beyond the hmanistic values they associate with it. This kind of appreciation is not so much wrong as partial, but it hinders a radical rethinking of the relation between Christian grace and art. Such readers are properly concerned with the Bible as "literature." If this is only a first step it is unobjectionable. Too often, however, the literature of the Bible is viewed in terms which obscure its radical distinctiveness. Such readers are often basically more attracted by its hieratic phrases, verbal resonance, and by their obscure personal nostalgias than by the naked sword of the text itself. Their case is like that of the lovers of Dante or Milton who lightly pass over the uncongenial theology, thus dismissing the integrity of the epic in question, to savor or glut themselves upon certain purple passages or other congenial sections. In the Bible they often turn to portions least alien to our Western mood — epic narrative, heroic or elegiac odes, sententious aphorisms. The long musical associations of the King James Version make it possible subtly to denature the original text. We are reminded of T. S. Eliot's comment on the translation of Baudelaire by Arthur Symons:

what came out was not Baudelaire but rather Swinburne.
This is not to say that the King James translators themselves were at fault.

C. S. Lewis, in a pamphlet, "The Literary Impact of
the Authorized Version," [12] has shown that the appreciation of this translation in terms of its "rhythm," "vigor,"
"grandeur," "nobility" is a relatively recent matter. He
ascribes it to the romantic movement and to "that taste
for the primitive and passionate which can be seen growing through nearly the whole of the eighteenth century." [13] Up to the late eighteenth century it was held
that the Authorized Version had a plain character which
called almost for apology. Tyndale wrote that the Scripture "speaketh after the most grossest manner," meaning
not what we would call indelicate but rather earthy. Mr.
Robert Jackson has studied what the various English
translators of the Bible wrote about their work, from
Tyndale to the translators of the King James Version.[14]
They were concerned with clarity and with variety of
diction (that is, they claimed the right to use different
synonyms in different places for the same Hebrew or
Greek term), but the reasons they give for any such
stylistic matters are always theological rather than literary.

We would not make too much of this warning against
a kind of Christian aestheticism. We merely take it as a
symptom which bears on the question of a well-grounded
Christian approach to the beautiful. Those who make
much of the Bible as literature are often really concerned
to underline their emancipation from theology. They
have good grounds often for disaffection with dogmatic
and literalistic use of Scripture, but neither should the
Bible be forced into narrowly humanistic or romantic
categories. The Authorized Version is vulnerable to such

misreading because its familiar cadences tend to numb
the attention and to create a spell which is easily confused
with spiritual elevation. W. H. Auden, in the Harvard
Phi Beta Kappa poem already alluded to, includes the
reading of the Bible "for its prose" among the prohibi-
tions. He classifies it with a variety of contemporary heresies, as follows:

> Thou shalt not be on friendly terms
> With guys in advertising firms,
> Nor speak with such
> As read the Bible for its prose
> Nor, above all, make love to those
> Who wash too much.[15]

There is a choice story by Rudyard Kipling dealing
with the King James Version.[16] As the story runs, Myles
Smith, one of the translators, is not satisfied with the work
done by his Oxford team on a portion of Isaiah, part of
the sixtieth chapter. The passage in question begins:

> Arise, shine; for thy light is come, and the glory of the
> Lord is risen upon thee

and closes with the lines:

> Thy sun shall no more go down; neither shall thy
> moon withdraw itself: for the Lord shall be thine ever-
> lasting light, and the days of thy mourning shall be ended.

But the translators had not yet achieved this consummate form. Smith, according to the story, sends his rough
draft of this section to a well-known actor and playwright
whose name happens to be William Shakespeare. Shakespeare, at a tavern, has the proof together with copies of

the same passage in the Latin, the Geneva Bible, Douai,
Coverdale, the Bishop's Bible and others. Shakespeare is
explaining to a companion, who happens to be Ben Jonson, how this all came about. The Reverend Myles Smith,
he says, has heard that

> I had some skill in words, and he'd condescend . . . to
> inquire o' me privily, when direct illumination lacked,
> for a tricking out of his words or the turn of some figure.

Shakespeare suggests to Ben Jonson that they do it together. Jonson reads out the Latin, and then Smith's draft
for the opening verses:

> Get thee up, O Jerusalem, and be bright, for thy light
> is at hand, and the Glory of God is risen upon thee. See
> how darkness is upon the earth and the peoples thereof.

Shakespeare exclaims: "That's no great stuff to put into
Isaiah's mouth!" Pacing back and forth in the orchard
of the inn, he then tries out word by word, phrase by
phrase — asking Ben Jonson for the readings of the various verses or the meaning of the Latin, selecting an as-
sonance here, rejecting a flat vowel there. I cite one
passage.

> He fell into the stage-stride of his art at that time, speak-
> ing to the air.
> "How shall this open? 'Arise?' No! 'Rise!' Yes. And we'll
> have no weak coupling. 'Tis a call to a City! 'Rise — shine'
> . . . Nor yet any schoolmaster's 'because' — because Isaiah
> is not Holofernes. 'Rise — shine; for thy light is come,
> and — !' 'And — and the glory of God!' — No! God's over-
> short. We need the long roll here. 'And the glory of the
> Lord is risen on thee.' (Isaiah speaks the part. We'll have

it from his own lips.) What's next in Smith's stuff? . . .
'See how'? Oh, vile — vile! . . . And Geneva hath 'Lo'?
(Still, Ben! Still!) 'Lo' is better by all odds: but to match
the long roll of 'the Lord' we'll have it 'Behold'. How goes
it now? *'For behold, darkness clokes the earth and —
and — '* "

So Shakespeare goes through the whole, and concludes
in a kind of ecstasy, as he repeats the sonorous cadences,
an ecstasy which takes the form of thumping his companion.

> 'If those other seven devils in London let it stand on this
> sort," he adds, "it serves. But God knows what they cannot
> turn upsee-dejee." Ben wriggled. "Let be!" he protested.
> "Ye are more moved by this jugglery than if the Globe were
> burned."

At the end Jonson says: "Who will know we had a part
in it?" To which Shakespeare replies: "God, maybe — if
he ever lay ear to earth. I've gained and lost enough —
lost enough."

I have cited this much of the story because it dramatizes
so well the difficulty we have after three centuries in distinguishing between our own conditioned reflexes to the
Authorized Version and the Scripture itself — between an
aesthetic response, and one that is more than aesthetic.
What is to us the infallibility of the diction of the King
James Version is probably very much a matter of sheer
familiarity.

3. The Plea for a Christian Discrimination

We have made a brief review of some of the historical
factors bearing upon the Christian or Protestant approach

to the arts. We return now to the new interest in what
is called "Christian discrimination," and this will lead
to our concluding discussion of what contribution can be
made to contemporary criticism growing out of Christian
insights. The task of "Christian discrimination" bears
upon all forms of art, highbrow and lowbrow, in which
the modern world makes itself known. The charter for
such activity is included in the biblical charge to "test
the spirits," to "discern the thoughts and intents of the
heart."

Nowhere do we have so concrete an opportunity to expose the truth and sophistry, the health and infirmity, of our
contemporaries, in all that concerns their values, loyalties,
and way of life, as in the novels they read, the plays they
see, the social symbols they revere, the dreams and fables,
indeed the myths which they feed upon. All this plays a
large part in the inner life, the color of the self, of the
modern individual, from the cultural model of the adult
to the hero-paradigm of the child. Here we have, to use a
phrase from Ezekiel, the "chambers of imagery" in the
heart. Needless to say, we have to deal here with the mass
media of the great public as well as with the traditional
arts, and all manner of cultural legacies. Moreover, the
confusions of the believer are often as open to correction
as are the confusions of those outside the church. What
is involved here is no less than a Christian criticism of
life, and no such task is possible without an appeal to theological insights as well as to aesthetic criteria. For the
church to confine its scrutiny of the world to social and
political matters is to forfeit engagement with the common life where error is even more deeply rooted, and
illusions more fatefully operative.

But Christian discrimination at work upon contemporary art forms will by no means be largely negative. Modern movements in the arts represent often a healthful protest against meagerness or vitiation in the spiritual life of the West, a witness to elements of the Christian tradition neglected by the church, as well as clues to a needed reformulation of the faith. The church must be hospitable to such insights, and furnish itself with groups qualified to mediate them to the rank and file of its members.

Yet a program of Christian discrimination labors against the suspicion that a partisan, a dogmatic motive may be at work. The theologian-critic presumably has an axe to grind, and converts to make! We have a good example of the outcry which any such activity may occasion. There is no more distinguished critic today than the Cambridge scholar F. R. Leavis. In his volume *The Common Pursuit*,[17] he includes a paper "The Logic of Christian Discrimination." He has in view two small volumes of criticism by Brother George Every, one of which is entitled *Christian Discrimination* [18] and the other *Poetry and Personal Responsibility*.[19] Every has been well-known as poetry critic for T. S. Eliot's quarterly, *The Criterion*. In the preface to the latter book, he writes:

> This book is intended as an introduction to contemporary poetry, considered as the sensitive spot in the modern mind, where a new response to life, a new outlook upon the world, is taking shape.

Brother Every assigns a high rank to certain Christian poets of today: Edith Sitwell, Norman Nicholson, Charles Williams, Anne Ridler. Professor Leavis accuses Every of "pushing his own special line of goods," and of mistaking expressions of the *Zeitgeist* for literature. Christian discrimination, he charges, "absolves Mr. Every from the literary critic's kind of discrimination." [20] The writers in question are heavily overrated, he thinks. Leavis is particularly severe on Charles Williams,[21] and he concludes his paper by remarking that Every represents the most active and formidable of contemporary gang movements.

We cite this little controversy as a warning to Christian discriminators. Leavis is unduly hard on Every. But any literary criticism which offers itself as "Christian" should be careful not to expose itself to the charge of being propagandistic. Any imperialistic approach to the arts on the part of the church will obscure aesthetic judgment and alienate the artist and the critic.

The sorry spectacle of literary polemic in France, involving the religious issue, should serve as further warning. Here Catholic writers like Massis and Mauriac have publicized their attempts to censor or to convert a Gide or a Cocteau. Fortunately, they have been called to order by their own fellow-believers. Thus the English critic Martin Turnell, himself a Catholic, writes on "The Function of a Catholic Critic." [22] He argues the general advantages of the Catholic position, but adds:

> The first thing a Catholic must realize is that in the literary order dogma must never be applied dogmatically. . . . We must be able to sympathize with the fresh experiences that are evolved in the course of civilization.[23]

What happens too often, he continues, is that partisanship perverts sensibility. This disability he assigns to such distinguished critics as Ferdinand Brunetière and Henri Bremond, and contrasts with theirs the exemplary critical method of Jacques Rivière.

The possible contribution of theologians to contemporary literary criticism is well illustrated by the work of

Fr. Martin Jarrett-Kerr, a member of the Anglican Community of the Resurrection. Under the pseudonym of Father William Tiverton, he published the highly appreciative study of D. H. Lawrence in 1951 to which we have already alluded. More recently, his *Studies in Literature and Belief* [24] have appeared. With all his interest in religious matters, what is significant here is that Jarrett-Kerr refuses to separate literature and belief, form and content, in the works which he analyzes. In each case, and his examples are taken from the whole sweep of European literature, he is interested in the way in which the form and style of the work are conditioned by the world-view of the author, how the general orientation of the artist is formative in the aesthetic achievement. He studies the transition of the Old English ballads from their pre-Christian to their Christian feudal versions, and assesses the subtle differences in the literary form and import of the two. He offers Calderon as an example of too external a Christian overlay, with resultant dramatic ineffectiveness. He discusses Manzoni, and the superiority of the genuine Catholic novelist to writers like Mauriac and Graham Greene, who stack their cards in favor of revelation.

> Mr. Greene's tawdry characters and stale scenery are evidently put there in a deliberately difficult obstacle race which the hero, grace, is to run — high-jumps made especially high to show his paces. [25]

Even the better Catholic novelists have this handicap, "that they are incapable of full-blooded doubt." Jarrett-Kerr, discussing the general problem, holds that literature and belief cannot be held apart, either in the work of the artist or of the critic. Man is one whole, and it is always the man in his entirety who expresses himself, whether in behavior, imagination, and dreams, or in language, imagery, and versification. The faith of a novelist, for example, is to be recognized not so much in passages dealing explicitly with belief, but "in his work as a whole, in his style, its imagery, its preoccupations, and his technique of novel-writing." In some way or other, a theological or ideological factor in a work of art is simply there in the form itself, and must be taken into account.

We could point to other instances where a theological approach to literature justifies itself as one concerned not with a facile didacticism but with a sound "poetic" and a strictly rhetorical approach. Just as Professor Yvor Winters has related moral to aesthetic criteria in the examination of modern writers, so Allen Tate has studied the subtle relation of personal outlook to aesthetic success in the work of Hart Crane. Professor Preston T. Roberts, Jr., of the Department of Literature and the Arts in the Divinity School of the University of Chicago, has carried out comparative studies of classical and Christian tragedy, with a similar integrity of approach.[26] A sizable list could be made of men and women today specially trained in theology who are urgently concerned with these matters. It is true that a critic does not have to be a theologian in a formal sense to enter into these dimensions of a work. What is worth noting is that the church is awakening in this respect, as in others, to the significance of the arts, and finding qualified representatives through which it can speak to the contemporary scene.

4. A "Christian" Aesthetic?

The danger of a dogmatic program of "Christian discrimination" with relation to the arts forces us back upon

the question of whether there can be such a thing as a
"Christian" aesthetic or a "Christian" poetic.[27] Certainly
not in a strict sense. We may admit that there is such a
thing as a Marxist criticism, in the sense that Marxist insights are employed by the critic, but there is hardly such
a thing as a Marxist aesthetic. Similarly, we may speak
informally of a Christian discrimination or criticism in
the sense that theological and biblical insights are invoked. But there is, properly speaking, no such thing as a
Christian aesthetic. If the term is used, it should be used
informally, to throw into relief the contributions that
can be made to the problem of aesthetic judgment by the
Christian understanding of man and the world. All critics
presuppose, or appeal to, one or another set of presuppositions. We have here an open market in ideas and in
criteria. In this sense, the theologian-critic takes his
chances with others, and seeks by persuasion to make his
case for the most adequate interpretation of literature.

It is especially the Protestant today who faces a problem
when he seeks to define the basis of artistic judgment.
This problem is illuminated when we look at the Catholic
dilemma. If Catholic moral theology owes too much to
Cicero, Catholic aesthetics owes perhaps too much to
Aristotle. The Thomist synthesis achieved a great result
in stamping the Gospel upon the best legacies of antiq-
uity, but thereafter suffers the embarrassment of being
permanently implicated in those legacies. The Reformation returned to the mood of "mortification of art" which
characterized the early church, and to the associated vigi-
lance in what concerns the life of the senses. But this
leaves the Protestants free to effect new combinations of
grace and nature.

Another way to define the difference is in terms of the
sacramental idea. The Roman doctrine of transubstantia-

tion in the Mass is the key to a Catholic art. It defines the relation of grace to nature, and the relations of the Catholic artist to the world. But this standpoint, in effect, disparages any "secular" art, in the good sense of that term. All art becomes "sacred art." Any truly significant work of a Catholic artist tends necessarily to revolve about Catholic themes. In reading the works of Catholic poets like Claudel and novelists like Bernanos, we sometimes find ourselves wishing that they would forget Christianity for awhile, take a moratorium on faith, and write as a bird sings — without doctrine. After all, the Bible itself contains secular and humanistic writings.

The doctrine of transubstantiation presupposes a very special metaphysic, a radical dualism between nature and the supernatural. The natural level, our human life, has no encounter with grace unless it is taken up into a massive objective sacral order which is essentially miraculous. In this context, it is true, the Christian symbol drawn from revelation has an immense prestige and authority. It belongs to the divine order. The very form of the symbol, as something objective and unchangeable, belongs to the divine order, in the same sense that the verbally inspired word of Scripture does for some Protestants. But this kind of Christian aesthetic is bought at a price. A Protestant approach to art, as we see it, is not bound to any one type of metaphysic. The distinction of grace and nature must, of course, be recognized. But the operation of grace in nature will not be objectified and localized in the same way. Grace has its incognitos through the whole sweep of human experience and talent.

In a recent book on the metaphysical poets,[28] an Anglican critic, Malcolm Ross . . . holds that "English religious poetry suffered a mortal blow when Protestant theology rejected the doctrine of transubstantiation, denied the 'real presence,' and allegedly cut off the created world, so that it could no longer be a valid bearer of the divine meaning." [29] Ross goes further in holding that poetry in general requires what he calls that "firmament of symbol" identified with this doctrine. Modern culture and modern literature are in dissolution because it has been denied. But the significance of art for the Christian, while it may require the doctrine of the Incarnation, need not rest upon the special doctrine of transubstantiation.[30] When a Catholic novelist or poet wishes to deal with the unbaptized raw material of our time, the fresh experiences of the modern world, he is in a difficult position. He can apply the Catholic Christian understanding of grace to such realities; but, if so, he is often charged with a dogmatic forcing of the material, as in the case of the work of Graham Greene, and Mauriac. Or he can secularize freely, so as to make possible a full encounter with the material, but in this case he lays himself open to the charge of heresy. Here the Catholic writer is in an analogous situation with the Catholic worker-priest. If he identifies himself too freely with the proletariat, he must be called to order. Charles Péguy's sympathies were so bound up with th unchurched, with those whom the church excluded from salvation, that he was obliged to remain on the threshold of the church.

More recently we have the case of Jean Cocteau, a Catholic, and yet not a Catholic. There is a clear witness that runs through all his vagaries, best expressed in his *Mystère laïc,* and in a letter to Maritain. The artist must deal with the "lay mystery," that is, with the secular experience understood religiously. But to deal with it, the artist must be free. What Cocteau says about the painter

Chirico fits exactly with Paul Tillich's understanding of the religious dimensions of much of the greatest post-impressionist painting. Chirico is "a religious painter without faith," "a painter of the lay mystery." With reference to Maritain, Cocteau writes: "I believe that art reflects morals, and that one cannot renew oneself without living dangerously and attracting slander. This is the only barrier between Maritain and myself." [31]

By "living dangerously" as an artist, Cocteau means dealing at first hand with the life beyond the fences of social or religious propriety. It is something like this that Wallace Stevens means when he says of the poet or the artist:

> The ephébe is solitary in his walk.
> He skips the journalism of subjects, seeks out
> The perquisites of sanctity, enjoys
>
> A strong mind in a weak neighborhood, and is
> A serious man without the serious. . . .
>
> He is neither priest nor proctor. . . .
>
> It is a fresh spiritual that he defines. . . .
>
> The actual landscape with its actual horns
> Of baker and butcher blowing, as if to hear,
> Hear hard, gets an essential integrity.[32]

Anglo-Catholicism does not appear to raise the same dilemma so sharply for the writer. In the poetry and plays of T. S. Eliot, for example, the Christian resources employed are so rich, and they are combined with such wise appreciations, that we find neither rigidity nor rebellion. The only exception is, perhaps, *The Cocktail Party*, for here many have felt that the dramatic effectiveness is limited by a certain dogmatic preconception.[33]

The great exfoliation of art about the Catholic faith is related to its sacramental conceptions. The Protestant position, with its different view of church and sacrament, and its emphasis on the ear rather than the eye, suffers greatly with respect to the whole realm of *sacred* art itself, but opens the door to the secular expression of the artist, just as it dignifies the secular vocations of men. In this sense art is liberated, though Protestantism has often, of course, chained the arts in its own way.

The Reformation Christian is perpetually on guard against idolatry, and therefore against assigning too great a prestige to the works of men's hands. He values the freedom of the spirit so much that he refuses to sanctify any given embodiments, to be fixated upon a static symbolism or expression other than the Scriptures — and even here it is not the word which is authority, but the Living Word within the word.

If the Protestant appears to disparage the life of the senses and sense representation, it should not be because of any intrinsic false asceticism, but because, in the Augustinian tradition, it is the relation between the individual soul and God which matters.[34] But this emphasis on religion as dynamic and personal does not exclude the uses of the imagination. It properly contributes vitality to the arts.

The dangers of this position are two: "angelism" and subjectivity. If the Protestant stresses the unpredictable and free action of the spirit and the Word at the expense of the incarnate media, then we have angelism, a false spirituality. The Protestant forgets that he is a creature immersed in a good creation. Or, on the other hand, if

he stresses the private, personal aspect of revelation, then
we have that erratic subjectivity and individualism of
which he is always accused by the Catholic. Here the
Protestant forgets the doctrine of the church. But neither
of these errors is intrinsic to Protestantism. Where present,
they arise largely from modern secular error.[35]

The Protestant emphasis on personal life and private
judgment opens the door to revolt and schism, it is true,
but also to creative vitality. It has been noted that several
modern literary forms, and especially the novel, resting
as they do upon a full exploitation of the psychological
life, have had a favoring setting in a Protestant culture.

Catholicism and Protestantism have both had their as-
sets and their liabilities in the aesthetic order. Protestantism can offer its shining examples in such figures as Milton and Bach, or in such expressions as the hymns of
Luther, the Negro spirituals, or the New England meet-
ing-house. Yet it has often lacked a proper Christian appreciation of the life of the senses. The Protestant theologian today has a chance to rethink the whole problem. He
will also insist on the autonomy of the arts.

A new Protestant approach thus carries with it the
emancipation of human vitality and personal richness.
In this respect, it will not disavow the great romantic impulse in the modern period. On the other hand, it will
know how to safeguard the humility of the artist, and the
health and sanity of his work. The artist is not a genius,
nor a God-intoxicated man, but a talent with a vocation.
The proper role of the hero of the novel or play is not
that of a Promethean hero nor a pathetic victim nor a
mere puppet of grace, but a servant of the purpose of
God. This does not rule out the creative inspiration of
the artist, and it does not rule out a sacramental view of

nature; but it does rule out idolatry, pagan mysticism, and magic. W. H. Auden has said these things effectively in his *Christmas Oratorio*. But to indicate the essential agreement of Protestant and Catholic theology at their best, we return in conclusion to Karl Barth's tribute to Mozart, as cited and paraphrased by Howard Schomer:

> Barth's theme was the freedom of Mozart. He rejoiced that in Mozart's music "the sun shines, but without burning or weighing upon the earth, and the earth also stays in place, remains itself, without feeling that it must rise in titanic revolt against the heavens." He bowed before an art in which "the laugh is never without tears, tears are never unrelieved by laughter." He honored Mozart, who, although Roman Catholic, and yet a Freemason, was utterly free of all institutional deformations, whether ecclesiastical or political. He confessed the reality and peace he finds in an art which embraces nature, man and God, which is as true to life as it is to death. . . . Mozart teaches us the sovereignty of the true servant.[36]

Chapter IV

The Cross: Social Trauma or Redemption

Odour of blood when Christ was slain
Made all Platonic tolerance vain
And vain all Doric Discipline.
　　　　W. B. Yeats, "Two Songs from a Play"

We think that this long night
This cold eclipse, is shade cast from Christ's
cross.
　　　　Elder Olson, *The Cock of Heaven*

1. Christ and the Psychologists

When poets and novelists deal with the Christ-story and the scenes and personages of the Gospels, they unconsciously modernize just as historians and theologians do and even more freely. They see Christ in their own image or in the image of their preferred life-ideal and make the Gospels a sounding board for their own philosophy and ethic. Churchmen do the same thing, but they are to some extent controlled by their training in the evangelical history and by their own particular patterns of sectarian tradition. Such patterns, diverse and dated as they often are, nevertheless rule out some forms of fanciful free-wheeling.

There is, indeed, a sense in which every significant portrayal of Christ must be a modernization. The "distance" between Nazareth and Detroit, between the first century and the twentieth, must be bridged. But re-portrayal should not be betrayal. Christ in modern dress is rarely convincing, though he has his incognitos in all times. The

93

best attempts to present him on the modern scene are the most indirect, as in the case of Georges Duhamel's superlative short story: *Élévation et mort d'Armand Branche*.[1] Here we have an allusive suggestion of Christ in the trenches in World War I which is all the more effective because it is not pressed. But the poet-Christ of Renan or of William Ellery Leonard, the antinomian oracle of Nietzsche and of Gide, the "man of genius" of Middleton Murry, the "Comrade Jesus" or socialist-Christ of the Marxists, the esoteric initiate of George Moore and now of Robert Graves, and the pacifist-anarchist of Faulkner's *Fable:* all such are modernizations which only show how we are led to delineate the past (as the future), each in terms of his own contemporary urgency. The unhappy result of this perennial practice is that in every decade we instruct Christ as to what he was and is, instead of allowing ourselves to be instructed by him.

The literary interpreter of the life of Christ, as one who waives usually both the relevant historical study and the theological tradition, is doubly vulnerable to the contemporary *Zeitgeist* in all spiritual matters. This means that as an intellectual he is more or less captive to the particular reigning science and its popularizers: in the current situation, psychology. As Darwinism produced its interpreters of Jesus and his influence, so more recently Freudianism has done the same thing, usually in conjunction with the influence of Sir James Frazer. First came the clinical demonstrations of the insanity of Jesus, which Albert Schweitzer answered definitively in his doctoral dissertation at Strasbourg. Then came the portrayals of the Nazarene healer as the first psychiatrist. More generally his saving death and resurrection have been fitted into a slot in this or that schema of redeemer-archetypes

provided by cultural studies in myth and ritual, and so
evacuated of any distinctive significance. The layman,
including the most sophisticated philosophers and social
scientists, notes that the terminology of seasonal fertility
rites and the symbols of gnostic regeneration occur in the
New Testament. But he has not recognized the decisive
underlying difference between *faith* based on revelation
through historical experience and *religion* based on nature
or on nature and the soul. What the cosmos can tell man
about ultimates — whether the constellations or the fer-
tility-cycles of living forms — is very little compared with
what man's social and moral experience can teach him.
And what the psyche and the spirit can teach in whatever
form of mysticism or seizure, exalting as it may be, is again
little as compared with the tuition of the heart and its
loyalties.

Thus the most common occasion for misconception of
Christ today among intellectuals lies in the new psychology, especially in social psychology. This confusion is,
however, abetted by the wide prevalence of morbid forms
of Christianity which justify the social psychologist at
many points.

These observations are preliminary to an examination
of one modern literary presentation of Christ, that of the
poet Robinson Jeffers in his poetic drama, *Dear Judas*.[2]
We are interested here in one particular slant which the
poet gives to the Gospel story, namely, his emphasis on
suffering as the clue to the appeal of Christ and of Christianity. It is at this point that we may identify a preoccupation on the part of the interpreter derived from modern
psychology. But we are also concerned with what to some
extent justifies Jeffers' emphasis on this point: a widespread heresy of Christians evident in exaggeration of

and even obsession with the Cross in its aspect of pain.

Through the centuries Christians have recurrently fallen into this kind of error. They have all too easily identified the Cross or the blood of Christ with mere suffering or let this motif play too large a part. What psychology sees on the one hand as masochism or on the other as sadism usurps an undue place in our understanding of the central event of Christianity. The consequences are seen in Christian art and ritual. Such a displacement of the real import of the Cross has its corollaries in various forms of sub-Christian asceticism, punitive attitudes, or self-punishment, and in orgiastic religious exercises. The dangers are not absent from forms of the faith which we think of as refined.

This question of the Christian's attitude to suffering is a fundamental one. What is at stake can be discussed in terms of contemporary literature. Jeffers presents the plausible but surely mistaken view — and the thesis in the work under examination can be found in his other writings — that Christ's empire over the hearts of men through the centuries rests upon the sheer fascination of agony and upon men's thinly veiled obsession with cruelty. Yet this writer and others may be partly excused for this view in the light of a good deal of Christian history. In any case the topic looked at in literary works offers the possibility of some significant Christian discriminations.

2. A Modern Lucretius

We take *Dear Judas* as our main text, but we may well give some prior attention to the work of Jeffers as a whole. Various factors combine to obscure the significance of his writing. Many readers are alienated by the violence and cruelty of the subject matter of his narrative poems. His unpopular political opinions openly voiced in his poetry have disaffected others. His art stands apart, moreover, from the kinds of poetry most appreciated in our period. Perhaps one feature of this isolation is to be found in his lack of inhibition in expressing a view and speaking in his own voice whether with respect to things political or more ultimate moralities. A reader of Jeffers should first free himself from any too limited definition of the art of verse, especially from the prestige of current critical opinion. He should then give his attention to the best of the narratives, which can be distinguished from those that are less successful. In the case of Jeffers this commonplace takes on a special importance. Finally the reader should allow himself to be interested in the philosophy of this poet, at least as an interesting option in our century for those who cannot accept the prevailing religious traditions but who are equally indisposed toward materialism and negation.

The position of Jeffers has, indeed, been identified with nihilism. This characterization is proper if it is recognized that he only rejects and denies in order to carry out his main role of celebrant all the more effectively. His affirmation is in terms of a kind of cosmic mysticism which must be distinguished from all usual forms of pantheism, an attitude which he calls Inhumanism. The final appeal of his often perplexing narratives lies in their dramatization of triumph, triumph of some life-principle or world-principle through wounds, mutilation, and agony. The best of them take on the character, at least in their climaxes, of hymns of salvation.[3]

The reputation of this twentieth-century Cassandra has

waned since the twenties, when he won extravagant testimonies from a number of outstanding critics. Attention has again been drawn to him since World War II by his version of the *Medea* of Euripides, which enjoyed a significant success in its New York production. A valuable new study of the poet has recently been published, *The Loyalties of Robinson Jeffers,* by Radcliffe Squires of the English Department of the University of Michigan.[4] This book, to which we are particularly indebted, dissipates many confusions about this California titan and his work, gives order to the various views that have been held about him and the influences that have been at work in his writing, draws clear lines between the better and the worse in the total output, and discusses reasonably the more controversial aspects of Jeffers' poetry and views.

There is no question that we have here an enormously talented writer and that as a figure in the cultural scene his stance and attitudes repay scrutiny. He illustrates the thesis that our nation will continue to produce its rebels and primitivists, its individualists of the frontiers (Jeffers identifies himself with "the West of the West") or the Big Woods or the Open Road, its new avatars of the American Adam uninitiated into law or church or restive under law and church, its Thoreaus and Whitmans, in every age. When this impulse is found in one so strongly marked with a Calvinist lineage it is doubly interesting. Radcliffe Squires' final category for Jeffers is that of a modern Lucretius, and this typing is illuminating, especially as it identifies well both the kind of cosmic *mystique* which finds expression in him and his scientific and rationalist leanings.

This writer's narrative poems are filled with violent actions, with unnatural crimes and with disgust of civili-

zation. He sees the disorder of his characters as a dramatization of our fallen condition. He proclaims his gospel
of Inhumanism — the glory of inhuman things which we
also may share. He states his case as follows:

> It seems time that our race began to think as an adult
> does, rather than like an egocentric baby or insane person.
> This manner of thought and feeling is neither misanthropic
> nor pessimist, though two or three people have said so and
> may again. It involves no falsehoods, and is a means of
> maintaining sanity in slippery times; it has objective truth
> and human value. It offers a reasonable detachment as a
> rule of conduct, instead of love, hate and envy. It neutral-
> izes fanaticism and wild hopes; but it provides magnifi-
> cence for the religious instinct, and satisfies our need to
> admire greatness and rejoice in beauty.[5]

Jeffers' father was a professor of Old Testament Literature in the Western [Presbyterian] Theological Seminary
in Pittsburgh. How many sons of talent born in the
church have departed from the family faith in our time,
yet always with some remaining indebtedness and distress.
Jeffers' sonnet "To His Father" contrasts movingly his
own lacerated lot with the serenity of the parent:

Christ was your lord and captain all your life,
He fails the world but you he did not fail,
He led you through all forms of grief and strife
Intact, a man full-armed, he let prevail
Nor outward malice nor the worse-fanged snake
That coils in one's own brain against your calm,
That great rich jewel well guarded for his sake
With coronal age and death like quieting balm.
I Father having followed other guides
And oftener to my hurt no leader at all,
Through years nailed up like dripping panther hides

For trophies on a savage temple wall
Hardly anticipate that reverend stage
Of life, the snow-wreathed honor of extreme age.[6]

Mr. Squires suggests that the grievous repudiation of
what his father had stood for plays its part in the deeper
imagery of the poems: especially that of "the destroying
prodigal." The relation to the church today of its alienated
sons is marked by ambivalence and is full of creative
stress. Even when Jeffers writes what reads like a parody
on the Gospel, namely his *Dear Judas,* it carries with it a
profound homage to the Christ.

Like many agnostics of today, Jeffers' thought has been
influenced by writers like Spengler. He sees the Western
world as well advanced on a final phase of emptiness and
internecine destruction. Civilization to him means death,
and has as its fruits both such sanguinary perversions and
crimes of individuals as abound in his tales, and modern
war on a world-scale as we have known it. His political
poems castigate the loss of freedom and of deep-rooted
religious integrity of the citizen. The poem "Shine, Perishing Republic" offers a good illustration:

But for my children, I would have them keep their
　　distance from the thickening center; corruption
Never has been compulsory, when the cities lie at
　　the monster's feet there are left the mountains.

And boys, be in nothing so moderate as in love of man,
　　a clever servant, insufferable master.
There is the trap that catches noblest spirits, that
　　caught — they say — God, when he walked the earth.[7]

In such passages we seem to hear the voice of the author's
Calvinist father. The doctrine of the Fall of man is indeed

no stranger to modern literature. We know that in some
disguise or other it recurs in writers like Faulkner, Eliot,
Auden, and Robert Penn Warren. Recognition of the
deceitfulness of the heart and its perennial masks of ego-
tism is a condition of salvation, personal and political.
This disabused view of man is one of the major distinctions
between Western Christendom and Communism. But it is
important that the arraignment of man be based on our
own self-knowledge rather than upon embittered contempt
for others. And everything depends also upon how the
Fall is understood — whether as a morbid dogma or as
a realistic appraisal.

Jeffers appears to see the evil in the world as conditioned by cycles. We live in the fall of an age, though men
are not therefore excusable. Salvation is to be attained
by "escaping the net," by transcending the common lot.
Symbols of the life of God are found in aspects of nature
that are wild and magnificent, alien and untouched by
man. For Jeffers, as for many men without religious belief in the usual sense, a door opens now and then beyond
human disgust and anguish upon an august reality, an
"all-heal," glimpsed especially in the ongoings of nature.
The poems celebrate such moments with impressive
power. For the rest, life is lived in a stoic endurance
which purges itself not only of hatred and envy but also
of the love of man. From the shorter lyrics or sketches,
"Their Beauty Has More Meaning" may be taken as
representative.

> Yesterday morning enormous the moon hung low on the
>   ocean,
> Round and yellow-rose in the glow of dawn;
> The night herons flapping home wore dawn on their wings.
>   Today

Black is the ocean, black and sulphur the sky,
And white seas leap. I honestly do not know which day is
　　more beautiful.
I know that tomorrow or next year or in twenty years
I shall not see these things — and it does not matter, it does
　　not hurt;
They will be here. And when the whole human race
Has been like me rubbed out, they will still be here: storms,
　　moon and ocean,
Dawn and birds. And I say this: their beauty has more
　　meaning
Than the whole human race and the race of birds.[8]

3. *Jeffers'* Dear Judas

Our main interest here, however, has to do with Jeffers'
attitude to Christ. We have seen that in the poem "Shine,
Perishing Republic" he refers to Christ as one who was
caught, like many of the "noblest spirits," in the trap of
the love of man. In *Dear Judas* we get the same theme.
Jesus is caught by the love of man. He thinks that as the
Son of God he will be able to save men by supernatural
means. Lazarus returned from the dead bids him disre-
gard the lot of men, which will only involve him in disaster. But Jesus perseveres. Lazarus, at the end of the
poem, says to Mary:

　　Your son has done what men are not able to do;
He has chosen and made his own fate. The Roman
　　Caesar will call your son his master and
　　his God; the floods
That wash away Caesar and divide the booty,
　　shall worship your son. The unconjectured
　　selvages
And closed orbits of the ocean ends of the earth
　　shall hear of him.[9]

It is Judas' role in the poem to betray Christ lest he occasion a Jewish uprising and a terrible Roman reprisal. Later Jesus comforts the conscience-stricken Judas by saying:

> Dear Judas, it is God drives us.
> It is not shameful to be duped by God. I have
> known his glory in my lifetime, I
> have *been* his glory, I know
> Beyond illusion the enormous beauty of the
> torch in which our agonies and all
> are particles of fire.[10]

But it is Jeffers' final view, as stated in one of his shorter poems, that Christ's way, his "insane solution" had

> . . . stained an age; nearly, two thousand years are
> one vast poem drunk with the wine of his blood.[11]

This reminds us of a recurrent view that the idea of the crucifixion, so deeply lodged in the Western consciousness, has given the Western people a lust of blood. We meet this idea in Yeats; in his poem "The Second Coming," for example:

> But now I know
> That twenty centuries of stony sleep
> Were vexed to nightmare by a rocking cradle.[12]

And Yeats refers again to this theme in the lines we have cited in our praescript from "Two Songs from a Play":

> Odour of blood when Christ was slain
> Made all Platonic tolerance vain,
> And vain all Doric discipline.[13]

Now what we have here is a very fundamental issue. There are not a few modern intellectuals who genuinely believe that Christianity, centering as it does in the Cross, has exerted its power by an appeal to, and indeed a secret stimulus to, man's hidden obsession with suffering and even blood-lust. They point to the popular piety and art forms of the centuries — crucifixes, paintings, and sculpture representing specifically the tortured Christ, as well as hymns, poems, and homilies dwelling in an ambiguous way upon the blood of Christ. It is not surprising that such observers find it difficult to draw the line between the healthy and the morbid. Psychology appears to speak all too relevantly of masochism and sadism. Social psychology speaks of repressions and ritual compensations, and of ancient archetypes of the atoning victim.

On such a view the crucifixion of Christ, like a blasting vision, was so vividly implanted in the imagination of believers that it has had a morbid effect on his followers in all generations; it disturbed what Yeats calls "Platonic tolerance" or the natural sanity of the Hellenic and humanist ideal; it acted as a kind of social or cultural trauma in the life of the West. Among the sophisticated, such a thesis would be related to deeper patterns of the scapegoat or sacrificial victim in ancient rites inspired by sanguinary delusions. The drama of the Cross would be seen as a main link in a long chain of enormities which testify to man's fatal propensity toward blood-lust or self-destruction.

It is not only in Yeats and Jeffers that one finds a connection established between the Cross and the sanguinary history of the Christian West. In the Book VII of Elder Olson's cycle of poems, *The Cock of Heaven,* we read:

> We think that this long night,
> This cold eclipse, is shade cast from Christ's cross.

And further:

> Cries one, "I study the hanged staring Man
> Strung like a hanged worm in spider-string;
> Foretell, thus, foulness; foul graves for Nero and
> Charlemagne,
> Crowned Frederick, gowned Gregory, Dolfuss, Fey,
> Stalin." [14]

Jesus as presented in Jeffers' *Dear Judas* recognizes that the power over mankind which will be his, will be achieved through suffering, and men's secret affinity for cruelty.

> Oh, power
> Bought at the price of these hands and feet, — and all
> this body perishing in torture will pay — is holy.
> Their minds love terror, their souls cry to be
> sacrificed for: pain's almost the God
> Of doubtful men, who tremble expecting to
> endure it, their cruelty sublimed. And I
> think the brute cross itself
> Hewn down to a gibbet now, has been worshipped;
> it stands yet for an idol of life and
> power in the dreaming
> Soul of the world. . . .
>
> I frightfully
> Lifted up drawing all men to my feet: I go a
> stranger passage to a greater dominion
> More tyrannous, more terrible, more true, than
> Caesar or any subduer of the earth
> before him has dared to dream of.[15]

And Christ predicts the "wasted valor of ten thousand martyrs" that will come after him:

> And men will imagine hells
> and go mad with terror, for so I have
>   feathered the arrows
> Of persuasion with fire, and men will put out
>   the eyes of their minds, lest faith
> Become impossible being looked at, and their
>   souls perish.[16]

There are many who, like Jeffers, see in what they call Cross-tianity a morbid ideal. One finds another example in Bernard Shaw. In the little book he wrote about the Bible called *The Adventures of the Black Girl in Her Search for God*,[17] Shaw charges the disciples with superstition and a "masochist Puritanism" which prepared the way for "all the later horrors of the wars of religion, the Jew burnings of Torquemada" and other atrocities. The crucifixion of Jesus, moreover, had, as he writes, the

> hideous result that the cross and the other instruments of his torture were made the symbols of the faith legally established in his name three hundred years later. They are still accepted as such throughout Christendom. The crucifixion thus became to the churches what the Chamber of horrors is to a waxwork: the irresistible attraction for children and for the crudest adult worshippers.[18]

The theologian is confronted in all such views with a major challenge. The scandal of the Cross is sharp enough without adding to it this unnecessary element. But there are undoubtedly many discerning men and women who misunderstand the Christian faith just at this point. They find it tainted with morbidity, and they are abetted in their error by widely current Christian attitudes and prac-

tices. It is, of course, true that the Christian faith relates
itself to a horrendous episode, the crucifixion of Jesus of
Nazareth, and that the event carries shock and revulsion
at many levels. It is true that there is a profound relation
between the theme of vicarious sacrifice in the Gospel and
ancient rites and myths dealing with expiation. It is true
also that Christianity has its own proper forms of asceticism and world-denial.

But the theologian can also make it clear that there is
no proper foothold in the Christian story for man's persistent or recurrent morbidity, his impulse to give pain
or to endure pain, his propensity for mortification and
maceration. If such traits have attached themselves to
Christianity in any of its forms, Catholic, Orthodox, or
Protestant, they are excrescences. Most often they represent
survivals of pre-Christian patterns, outcroppings of primitive legacies, or corruptions of Christian piety occasioned
by contemporary cultural factors. Dr. John Mackay has
well documented this in connection with Latin American
Catholic practices as well as some forms of Spanish Catholic art and mysticism. Writing about Miguel de Unamuno
he says:

> [Unamuno] makes the luminous suggestion that in the
> Spanish religious tradition there have been two repre-
> sentative views of Christ. . . . One Christ is the "Recumbent
> Christ of Palencia," who is utterly dead; the other is the
> "Crucified Christ of Velasquez," who never ceases to ago-
> nize. The Recumbent Christ of Palencia . . . is an utterly
> dead figure, a veritable mass of death. The gruesome image
> represents Christ taken down from the cross, gory and
> pallid. "This Christ . . . will never rise again." On the other
> hand, there is in the Spanish religious tradition what
> Unamuno would call the *Agonizing Christ of Velasquez.*
> . . . His viewpoint recalls that of Pascal for whom Christ

"will continue to be in agony until the end of the world."
. . . The Christ of Velasquez, like the cross which Unamuno
drew across his heart, is the symbol of his endless struggle.
. . . As a follower of this Christ, he does not ask for light
or peace, but only for water, water from the abyss, to give
him strength to maintain the struggle. The only peace he
asks for is "peace in Christ's struggle," "peace in the midst
of war." [19]

The cases of Pascal and Unamuno (appealing to Velasquez) indicate that there is an irreproachable sense in
which the suffering of Christ can be stressed and even be
viewed as lasting until the end of time. As one moment
or station in the contemplation of Christ, this concentration on the agony may be seen as essentially Christian,
provided always that it gives way promptly to the theme
of Resurrection and Victory. A hyperbolic or baroque
artistic expression of this moment of the agony may well
be expected in the Spanish mystical tradition. At the
same time such forms of piety are overstrained, and easily
pass over into forms that are more than suspect, as is evident in other aspects of Spanish Catholicism and especially
in Latin America. The Passion of Christ ended on Good
Friday. No doubt the Risen and Triumphant Christ
shares in the continuing struggle of the Church Militant
and the martyrs. The deeper sense of this is that God
himself is not impassible but is afflicted with all our afflic-
tions. But the secret of the suffering of the Christian is
that it is indissolubly merged with joy: "suffering but
always rejoicing," what Luther called *Kreuzzeligkeit*. To
leave this out is to fall back into heathenism and into the
"sorrow of the world" which "worketh death." "For as we
share abundantly in Christ's sufferings, so through Christ
we share abundantly in comfort too."

One consideration is highly important here. The accounts of the Passion of Christ in the Gospels themselves are devoid of any sentimental or morbid features. The Evangelists do not present the episodes of Christ's last hours in such a way as to harrow or exacerbate the feelings of the reader. The scenes are presented with a great austerity. This is related to the fact that the Gospels are not biographies or martyrologies or even tragedies. Their purpose is not to set forth the death of a hero or a martyr. They portray a divine transaction whose import far transcends the feelings of the protagonist or the sensibilities of the observer. What is important for the Evangelists is the revelation mediated — the operation of God in the event — not the poignancies of the occasion.

Our modern sentiment loves to linger over the crown of thorns or the flagellation. But our best understanding of *koine* Greek usage today makes it doubtful whether the plant in question, the *akantha,* had any sharp spines. The crown of acanthas was placed on the head of Jesus, just as the purple robe and mock scepter were used, for purposes of ridicule, not to inflict pain. This was the garb of royalty. As for the flagellation, it is mentioned only in a passing phrase. The interest of the Evangelist here is in the fulfillment of prophecy and in the due preliminaries of Roman crucifixion.

Thus our primary Christian sources show the way. The Cross of Christ should be a fountain of health and not of morbidity. The representation of the Passion of Christ in art should not encourage the gratification with pain which is so widely evident in certain forms of Latin-American art. The blood of Christ should not be dwelt on in cult or hymn or sermon in such a way as to feed men's regressive impulses toward excitement and self-mortification, as it is in some forms of Protestant orgiastic practice.

There is indeed a deep mystery in the Cross, and the agony of Christ is related to the law of suffering which runs through the whole story of life, human and sub-human. Here is one aspect of the fascination that the Cross exerts upon all beholders. This is one meaning of the words: "I, if I be lifted up, will draw all men unto me." A God without wounds can never hold men long. Robinson Jeffers recognizes this scarlet thread of blood and agony that runs through all of life. For him it is the lot even of those who escape the net of life and attain to the tower beyond tragedy.

But if Christ "reigns from the tree" his dominion rests on much more than sheer suffering. In the Christian story, the Passion of Christ is only important as the final link between the love and righteousness of God and the ac-tualities of our human lot. What is important here is not the subjective suffering of Christ, but the objective intervention of God in the whole drama of death and victory. The attention of the beholder passes on beyond the marks of the Passion to recognize the cosmic trans-action in course and the claim made upon him by it. Here is the leverage by which grace takes effect on the human condition and by which "mercy, pity, peace, and love" come to make the earth their dwelling-place.

So understood, the death of Christ, and blood of Christ, cannot evoke what Yeats calls turbulence and intolerance in the sequel. The only shadow that the Cross casts over history is one of shelter and asylum. If the legacy of the crucifixion has been compounded with sanguinary delu-sions in the annals of mankind, the fault is not with the Gospel. And in rejecting such perverted versions of Chris-tianity, modern skepticism may play a useful part.

Chapter V

Faulkner and
Vestigial Moralities

. . . He went his way
Down among the Lost People like Dante, down
To the stinking fosse where the injured
Lead the ugly life of the rejected.
W. H. Auden, "In Memory of Sigmund Freud"

1. Religious Folkways and the Agnostic

At no point is the gulf wider between the church, or a large part of it, and the modern intellectual, than in the area of moral behavior and its presuppositions. We have in mind not ethics alone, but that region where morals, values, manners, and taste all overlap. Appropriate conduct is, indeed, very much a matter of imagination, of spiritual tact, of sensitive perception. The greatest handicaps to creative social behavior are rigidity and obtuseness. In religious groups these are often encouraged by moral dogma and habit. In this area, the agnostic today, as over against the church, is not only emancipated and indifferent; he is caustic, if not vituperative.

The church's moralities often take on a desiccated character, involving taboos and tyrannies which appear cruel and wasteful. They are associated with attitudes and appreciations, or rather lacks of appreciation, which have called forth satire and exposure from a long line of modern writers, from Blake to Ibsen, Shaw, Lawrence, and

Joyce. Sometimes it is the private costs of such rigidities in the institution of the family, and in the life of the sexes, which is attacked.[1] Sometimes it is a dismal asceticism and cult of ugliness, or the dearth of courtesy, decorum, and ceremony in life. Sometimes it is the social immoralities of caste and irresponsible wealth, as sanctioned by religion.

It is especially in the novel that such probings of pernicious codes is effectively carried out. The novelist dealing with authoritarian societies, Puritan or feudal or totalitarian, can have a field day in combing out the strands of evil which blight the family and the individual, the noxious legacies which represent fate for every new generation. The emancipated individual today, the rebel against what he sees as stultified convention, looks on all such moralities with a clinical detachment. In Faulkner's *Absalom, Absalom* this attitude is well described; LeBon, we are told, apropos of his own unconventionality,

> now found Sutpen's action and Henry's reaction a fetish-ridden moral blundering which did not deserve to be called thinking, and which he contemplated with the detached attentiveness of a scientist watching the muscles of an anaesthetized frog — watching, contemplating them from behind that barrier of sophistication, in comparison with which Henry and Sutpen were troglodytes.[2]

The particular moral situation which occasions this judgment, one that involves LeBon's octaroon mistress, is a highly complex one. We may not suppose that the views of Faulkner himself are to be identified either with the emancipation of LeBon or with the particular moralism of the Sutpens, father and son. But Faulkner's work certainly illustrates the demand made upon Christians, that they re-examine their moralities at least once in a millennium. No doubt sophistication in these matters may be in error as well as convention, but sophistication is essential.

The modern critic of religious folkways finds himself supported by the new sciences of man as well as by a kind of secular conscience. This secular conscience itself rests back upon the religious tradition, although the critic may not be aware of it. The modern agnostic writer is often unconsciously appealing to a living religious tradition against one that is moribund, and he has often not discovered that important elements in the church today agree with him. Attacks on Christian patterns of life may indeed be rooted in positivist or hedonist presuppositions. We are not defending these. Nor are we defending those attacks which are inspired by dogmatic Marxism or by a fascist mentality or by sheer personal bitterness in the writer, which often takes on a Marxist or a fascist disguise. We are concerned with better grounds and with indictments which direct themselves not at Christian faith itself but at its distortions and betrayals.

The urgency today of a re-examination of Christian codes and moral attitudes is pressing. The great masses of men are baffled by the issues of conduct and decision. They are caught in new circumstances for which older prescriptions offer no guidance. They feel themselves under constraints whose authority they no longer recognize, and caught in social patterns which dwarf them and which breed hostility and frustration. Literature often uncovers these tangles more discerningly than moral theology. The churchman is handicapped in this area just because established attitudes have become second nature to him. The modern agnostic has felt the full brunt of the contemporary crisis, and has suffered shocks which have awakened him from the spell of habitual conformity. Not in a mood of bravado, but in one of anguish, he finds himself under the necessity of coming to terms on his own and without benefit of clergy with his own moral and spiritual dilemmas.

His situation is indeed parlous — and this reflects itself in the desperate note in much modern literature — for he finds himself estranged from the usual securities, deprived of solid footing and pushed toward nihilism. He becomes, as it were, the scapegoat of a social situation, of a *kairos,* but for that very reason his work can become revelatory. At great personal cost he becomes a pathfinder toward a new morality and a new order.

In a period of cultural change like that in the midst of which we stand, the great task is that of a reconception of the Christian ethic. But a prior problem is that of the lag of outworn moralities, the stubbornness of inherited and indurated attitudes which are no longer relevant, and which have often themselves become baneful rather than healthy. We may think, for example, of certain aspects of the New England Puritan tradition, or of the Southern cultural tradition. Even those who are intellectually emancipated are often still unconsciously motivated and ruled by such patterns: by mechanisms which are stronger than they are; by legacies of a sound tradition which have become destructive rather than helpful, negative rather than positive. There is a Puritan granite which strengthens, but there can be a Puritan granite which crushes. There is a Southern way of life which nourishes, and there is one which strangles.

William Faulkner sees these issues, the problem of a decadent or otiose order — the curse of a vestigial code.

His exploration of such themes has its favoring setting in the Southern scene, and other Southern writers have wrestled with it from this point of vantage. But the issues raised have a universal bearing. The codes in question are, at the same time, social and religious, and so far as religious codes are involved, there is no separation of ethic from sanction; that is, theology itself is involved as well as behavior.

Among the many charges brought against modern writers, including Faulkner, by their critics is the charge that they avidly scent out extreme aspects of human corruption and dredge up such instances of depravity and violence as may lend their work a spurious shock appeal, or pander to men's secret urge toward cruelty. There are such writers and they should be condemned. But such criticism may arise from an unduly fastidious or genteel habit of mind, one that cloaks a deep fear of reality. Art must relate itself to the whole compass of life. It must not drape reality, though it should clothe it, in the sense of seeing it in context. So far as the unflinching portrayal of evil goes, we have to make distinctions among modern writers. We may note that the best of them are in good company under this head if we look back at the world's classics, that the important test is not one of the kind of subject matter but the way it is treated — and by *proper way* here we do not mean a shallow, moralizing one. We may add that much of the most significant theology today speaks of the "boundary situation" in life as the necessary focus of revelation and redemption. The boundary situation is no mere abstract point of tangency between creature and creator, but that locus of freedom where the diabolical and the divine are joined in dramatic conflict. Unsavory episodes and situations are the outcome of

private complacencies and passions, and they afford
unique opportunity for the scrutiny of life as a whole.
As Karl Barth has said, "Life emerges at the point of
mortification." And Yeats: "Test act, morality, custom,
thought in Thermopylae."

But we are concerned here with a special aspect of this
charge that modern writers revel in evil. It is pointed out
that figures like Proust, Joyce, Kafka, Eliot are preoccu-
pied with subjectivity, with, psychologism. Modern literature and art represent a kind of psychoanalytic activity,
and what is more, they are actuated by an impulse to
unmask human nature and disparage it. The public man,
the civic man, is no longer interesting. In a mass society
he has lost his freedom and responsibility. Only the Marxist artist has been interested in social man, and this for
reasons of propaganda. Indeed, we hear it said that it is
not only literature and the arts today that are dominated
by psychologism. The same is true of philosophy and
religion. Existentialism in particular starts out with man,
the individual or generic man, and has only a secondary
interest, if any, in the world or the public order.

Now the present moral situation may go far to explain
this obsession with inwardness, but our special interest
here is to note that accusations of psychologism and denigration of man are not in order so far as Faulkner is
concerned. With whatever finesse he scrutinizes the
human heart, it is always with a full awareness of the
historical and social context. He is not only an analyst,
but a moralist and a social moralist. He is interested not
only in a locale, but in a region, the South; not only in a
region, but in a "Way of life," and in ways of life; and not
only in one generation, but in many generations in their
interlocking continuity. And instead of denigration or

reveling in evil, what we have is rather — along with a Brueghel-like gift for satire and the grotesque — a persistent, urgent, and delicate scrutiny of the moral forces by which men endure, and the transcendent factors by which they are saved.

2. The Sound and the Fury

We propose now to examine in some detail Faulkner's novel *The Sound and the Fury*,[3] giving attention especially to the portrayal here of the breakdown of an inherited order, the decline and fall of the Compson family — a rotting family in a rotting house — all representative of a wider cultural fatality. We are interested especially in the implicit critique of Christian elements in the society presented. We shall find supplementary clues in other writings of the author. Since we are dealing with novels, we do not assume that we hear Faulkner speaking in the voice of his characters. None the less, we identify intimations and values in the fable which he has ordered, and we identify laws in the drama he has conceived. It is the myth that speaks to us through Faulkner, not Faulkner who preaches to us through a contrived tale.

In this fable we find ourselves part of a run-down Southern family, all of whose members are, it is said, "poisoned." The action takes place, for the most part, in the first quarter of this century, but the incubus of the past is formidable. The cast is well-known: the dipsomaniac father; the querulous mother, an invalid; the several children, including the idiot Benjy, whose phantasmagoric stream of consciousness gives us part of the story. Then there are the Negro servants, including Dilsey: drudge, cook, nurse, who keeps two sinking families afloat, the one white and the other her own.[4] We see the meager and irremediably injured early years of the children, the prenatal history, as it were, of later giant traumas and obsessions; the inculcation of social and racial distortions; the inbreeding of desiccated, feudal-Christian survivals in the son Quentin. We see the blasting from the start of the delicate filaments of adolescent bloom in his doomed sister, Candace (or Caddy), whose later dereliction represents sheer despair rather than rebellion. We see this theme repeated in *her* daughter, who, as she flees from the family to her lover, cries: "Whatever I do, is your fault. If I am bad, it's because I had to be. You made me. I wish I was dead. I wish we were all dead." [5] Incidentally, let us note here that Faulkner does not finally see his doomed characters as mere puppets. In the case of the similar heroine, Temple Drake, in *Requiem for a Nun,* she herself asserts over and over again her own complicity, "because," as she says, "Temple Drake liked evil." [6]

But to return to *The Sound and the Fury:* the story moves on to the suicide of Quentin, and to the later period when his brother Jason becomes the head of the family and the agent of its final extinction and dispersion.

But our interest is especially in the son Quentin, in whose monologue in the hours preceding his suicide as a Harvard student, we find the best documentation on the deeper, tangled roots of the family calamity. We find in this section the same agonized, sardonic interior monologue which we have come to recognize in *The Waste Land,* in parts of *Ulysses,* and in other revealing transcripts of the modern consciousness. Windows are opened for us upon radical alienation and estrangement, upon a private inferno. Excruciating reminiscences alternate with even more tormenting echoes of vanished felicity (moments of childhood — hunting episodes — lines of great poetry). Reveries of nostalgic beatitudes are punctuated by motifs of horror and putrefaction; re-enacted shame is accompanied by blasphemies and maledictions. We look into a landscape of molten lava and fumes, the purlieus of dissolution. Yet evident throughout the monologue, as an ultimate sounding board, is an imprescriptible moral order or criterion, without which there would be no spiritual torment, no revulsion, and no flight from time. Yet this valid order is confused with false authorities, with a usurping superego or tyrannical social code, so that valid and invalid claims are hopelessly intertwined.

The consummate art and wisdom of Faulkner appear here, above all, in his success in making the self-destruction of the student convincing, and in lending verisimilitude to the act and its motives and antecedents, and to the extended monologue which accompanies it. This means that the author must show us convincingly both the personal, psychic derangement and the relation of this to the family history, as well as the more general cultural determinants. These factors can be distinguished as the role of his father, his intimate relation to his sister Caddy, and the ghostly social and religious patterns he was bred to.

When Quentin graduated from high school, his father gave him the watch which he himself had received from his own father; "Quentin, I give you the mausoleum of all hope and desire, I give it to you not that you may remember time, but that you might forget it now and then for a moment, and not spend all your breath trying to conquer it. Because no battle is ever won," he said. "They are not even fought. The field only reveals to man his own folly and despair and victory is an illusion of philosophers and fools." [7] When the son got up on the morning of the day in which he would take his own life, he broke the glass of the watch and twisted off the hands — but, even so, he could not help hearing the ticking. Another thing he remembered his father saying was that "Christ was not crucified: he was worn away by a minute clicking of little wheels." The preoccupation with mechanical time, which runs all through Quentin's long monologue, is highly significant. It exalts by contrast what Faulkner often recurs to: the health associated with intuitive, natural, organic, uncorrupted rhythms.

Two critics have dealt in interesting ways with the concept of time in this novel. Peter Swiggert [8] sees Quentin as a victim of the false romantic attitude of a decadent South to its past. On this view, the present is cut off from the past, the past is unredeemable. Clock time only reinforces this despair. Swiggert appeals to Allen Tate, who contrasts duration measured by a "logical series" with a more responsible view of time, in which life is accepted "as from a religious or atemporal perspective." Such a view characterized the Christian South at its best, and by such a view of time and life Quentin was hopelessly haunted. On such a view, the past, whether of the group or of the individual, is redeemable. We may say that Faulkner himself is to be identified with such a Christian view of time. The whole positive meaning of the sequence of novels, *Sanctuary* and *Requiem for a Nun,* is expressed in the words of Gavin Stevens, "The past is never dead. It's not even past." [9]

Jean-Paul Sartre has an interesting paper on our present topic.[10] He notes that for Quentin, as it is said: "time is your misfortune" — in the sense of past time. Quentin knows no living presence of freedom, and therefore no future. Even his imminent suicide is presented as already accomplished. Sartre cites the lines: "I am not is, I was." The order of the past is the order of the heart — hence the absurdity of clocks. A man is defined as the "sum of his past" and nothing more, and the past is an accumulation of fortuitous rubbish. As Quentin's father put it:

Man, the sum of what have you. A problem in impure properties carried tediously to an unvarying nill: statement of dust and desire.[11]

Sartre rightly objects to this view of time. He holds to the idea of real freedom and real future in his familiar existentialist terms, but he wrongly identifies Faulkner's views with those of Quentin. He contrasts Faulkner and Proust. With regard to the past, Proust would remember it all; Faulkner would forget it — in favor of mystical, ecstatic escapes. Sartre ascribes a thorough-going doctrine of despair to Faulkner, but prefers his own version of this. But Sartre has entirely misconstrued Faulkner, and that through the ingenuous error of identifying the author with one or more of his characters. The whole fable of *The Sound and the Fury* points toward a healthful order of values which has been violated.

Quentin's relation to his sister Caddy is the decisive factor in his disarray and self-destruction. In her corruption the doom of the family and his own impotence to help are brought home to him most intolerably. She was the only human creature from whom he had received any sustenance throughout his meager and blocked childhood. This meant that his relationship with her was inevitably intense and obsessive, and that he was vulnerable to incestuous fantasies, at least in retrospect — fantasies which

served as a pretext for guilt. He could persuade himself
that he had initiated his sister's demoralization. His feeble
attempts to drive off her lovers or to convince her that
they were scoundrels had no effect; but, as Faulkner makes
clear, he did not really love her. Like all the children, he
had been rendered all but incapable of love. He loved
"the idea of chastity in her," as Faulkner tells us, "some
concept of Compson honor." And so far as Caddy loved
him, what she loved in him — again, as Faulkner explains
in his appendix — was "the bitter prophet and inflexible,
corruptless judge of what he considered the family's honor
and its doom." [12]

But the inherited religious criterion played a significant part here too — a religious legacy so denatured that
it operated for destruction. Quentin so far warped the
idea of guilt and penalty as to seek damnation for his
sister and himself, dramatizing his suicide as a retribution
for both. As Faulkner states it, he

> loved not the idea of incest, which he would not commit,
> but some Presbyterian concept of eternal punishment: he,
> not God, could by that means cast himself and his sister
> both into Hell, where he would guard her forever and keep
> her forevermore intact amid the eternal fires.[13]

This meant that in his own fatal solitude Quentin had to
take her with him into the negative salvation of his own
suicide and escape from time. But the whole drama in his
mind was clothed about with a borrowed or vestigial
Christian crime-and-punishment ideology.

All this is not so strange as may at first appear. We are
aware of the fact that there are people whose lives are
undernourished and who are impelled to punish themselves or to flout their own best opportunities for a better

life — to court persecution or ascetic poverty or ugliness
— as perhaps the only way open to them to feel important
or to gain identity, or achieve some intensity of personal,
consciousness. And all this can be cloaked under religious
sanctions, and carried out in Christian terms of pseudo-
martyrdom, re-enactments of the Cross, orgiastic or refined.

The tragedy of Quentin Compson is conditioned on the
one hand by a social code of Southern chivalrous honor
and womanhood, and by a truncated Christian conception
of guilt and retribution, severed from all ideas of grace:
law without grace. We have an inverted vestigial nobility
or chivalry — ultimately a Christian order — which is
powerful for destruction rather than for health, and it is
powerful for destruction because it is fed by the main
taproot of biological vitality. The cables carrying the
powerful life-impulse, as in all men, provide here in re-
verse the strength of the death-wish.

Thus Faulkner as moralist is exposing all the mechanisms, social as well as psychological, which represent the
destructive element in his society, and in other forms in
all societies. We find a warning against inveterate social
tyrannies, the incubus of inherited and desiccated cultural
ideals and patterns: obsessive vestigial codes and rigidities, whether associated with ideas of honor or caste, with
social authority, status, or manners, with sexual deport-
ment or economic activity. We find also a warning against
fossilized religious sanctions, conceptions, or rituals,
which, detached from their healthful or vital sources, become malign tools of social control, thus lending a specious absolute authority to inhuman usages. And such
religious axioms and norms are all the more dangerous
because they are bred into the unconscious life of new

generations. One of the most obstinate elements in social evil is represented by its inverted Christian components: inverted guilt conceptions, inverted asceticisms, inverted sacrificial impulses.

We have in this area a good illustration of the considerations which lead many perceptive moderns to withhold allegiance from some forms of institutional religion and religion generally. They have had personal experience of a negative or an ambiguous operation of religiosity in persons or groups that they have known. When pseudo-Christian attitudes and codes are part of the malign social stream in which individuals have lost their freedom to impersonal group authorities, we can understand the bitter ejaculation of Quentin, citing his father:

> All men are just accumulations, dolls, stuffed with sawdust, swept up from the trash-heaps where all the previous dolls had been thrown away. The sawdust-flowing from what wound in what side that not for me died not.[14]

Quentin says that men are puppets and that the death of Christ for such men and for himself makes no sense to him. Quentin, in this situation and with his acquaintance with Christianity, could say this, just as Joyce could say something like it in *The Portait of the Artist as a Young Man,* out of the same truncated experience with another Christian tradition.

The kind of diagnosis of culture and religion which occurs in fiction like that of Faulkner is far more searching and illuminating than is possible in other media. The form of the modern novel encourages presentation of many dimensions and levels and facets of reality. Sociological analysis, with all its advantages, confines itself to particular tools and methods. The social prophet or revolutionary — a Saint-Simon, a Proudhon, or a Marx — combining moral vision with acute discernment, forfeits one great advantage: that of presenting social reality in terms of living persons and their interrelations. The novelist can carry his portrayal of human life down into the deeper roots of motive and action, and deal with the hidden jungle in ways not open even to the psychologist.

One can illustrate this in connection with the history of modern anti-Christian polemic. The critics of Christianity from the time of Celsus have often been severe on the church; even when their own position has been heretical, they have none the less made it sensitive to its errors. But the value of such criticism depends upon its cogency. Compared with such analysis in depth as the one that Faulkner affords, the older, familiar charges against secularized Christianity are superficial. By such older charges I refer to the orthodox Marxist reproach against it, that it is escapist and other-worldly — that it lulls the exploited into acceptance of their lot, and discharges the conscience of the powerful classes of their real responsibility. Or the Nietzschian reproach against Christianity, that it condones and flatters the unheroic and fosters a slave morality. Such polemics have had their validity and have had fateful historical influence. But such analyses of Christianity have been ideological rather than dramatic, and their impact has been correspondingly limited. A disclosure in dramatic terms of attenuated Christian society, such as we find in novels like those of Faulkner or Dostoievsky or Gide, brings the issue home to us in a far more urgent manner.

No doubt the Freudian challenge to Christianity is more subtle and pressing than those of Marx and Nietzsche. But even here, the probing of the artist and the novelist gives a greater sense of reality and due complexity than the approach of the scientific analyst. The scientist is more limited in his field of operation. He works from a confessedly partial perspective, with tools adapted to a selective observation. Faulkner, like many other creative writers of our time, is immeasurably indebted to modern psychology. But the total picture of man which emerges in his novels offers more inclusive insights than one finds in the clinic.

3. Grace and Its Disguises

We have given primary attention to the exposure of perverted and festering moralities in Faulkner — moralities that had formerly been healthful: "Lilies that fester smell far worse than weeds." But Faulkner can also present the other side of the shield of Christianity. In *The Sound and the Fury,* we find this significantly in the last section, in the account of the church service of the Negroes, and of the sermon of the colored preacher from St. Louis, the Rev'un Shegog. This whole episode stands out in the novel like the corresponding sermon in the whalemen's chapel in *Moby Dick.* Faulkner sets forth the life-giving mystery of the Christian faith here among the poor in spirit over against the riddle or even curse which religion may represent for most of the more cultured whites.

The meaning of the Negro service emerges especially in the person of the old, enduring servant of the Compsons, Dilsey. This colored slavey, nurse, confidant, and foster-mother — battered and buffeted — has, as we have said, kept the swamping raft of the household afloat, has absorbed in herself the grievances and hostilities of all through the daily wear and tear and throughout periodic disasters. The religious service discloses to us where she gets what she calls "de comfort en de unburdenin," and the meaning to her of what the Rev. Shegog appeals to as "de recklickshun en de blood of de Lamb." We have a good example here of how the dangerous theme of blood and atonement can be understood in a healthy and not a masochistic way, even in an uncultured group.

The preacher evokes "de blastin, blindin, sight" of Calvary, and "de turnt away face of God," and warns the rapt congregation that God can turn his face away from men:

> I can see de widowed God shet His do'; I sees de whelmin flood roll between; I sees de darkness an de death everlastin upon de generations.[15]

One could almost say that these words of the preacher sum up the landscape of evil which Faulkner presents throughout the changing scenes of the novel: "I see de darkness an de death everlastin upon de generations." But the preacher goes on:

> Den, lo! Breddren! Yes, breddren! Whut I see? Whut I see, Oh sinner? I sees de resurrection en de light; sees de meek Jesus sayin Dey kilt Me dat ye shall live again; I died dat dem whut sees en believes shall never die. Breddren, oh breddren! I sees de doom crack, en hears de golden horns shoutin down to glory, en de arisin dead whut got de blood en de recklickshun of de Lamb! [16]

As Dilsey is walking away from the service, her daughter bids her stop weeping.

"Why'nt you quit dat, mammy?" Phrony said, "Wid
all dese people lookin. We be passin white folks soon."
"I've seed de first en de last," Dilsey said, "Never you
mind me."
"First en de last whut?" Phrony said.
"Never you mind," Dilsey said, "I seed de beginnin en
now I sees de endin." [17]

Dilsey has seen the beginning and the ending in two
senses: the beginning and the ending, the first and the
last, in the sense of Christ as Alpha and Omega; but also
the beginning and the ending of the long tragedy of the
last generation of the Compsons. For just that morning
the granddaughter, Quentin, had run away with the con-
cealed wealth of her uncle Jason, and this act entails the
disasters that follow, the death of the mother, the incar-
ceration of Benjy, and dispersal of the family.

Christianity in its uncorrupted aspects appears in other
novels of Faulkner, and is not only identified with the
lowly Negro, or, as in *The Fable,* with a disesteemed element from the lower strata of society. In *Requiem for a
Nun,* the sequel of *Sanctuary,* we have one of the most
authentic and searching Christian dramas in modern
literature. Its focus on husband, wife, and family and
the agony of the modern household sets it beside Eliot's
Family Reunion. It offers us a study in pride and contri-
tion, in vicarious sacrifice and forgiveness; and includes
the Negro slavey, the "demon nun," but also the college-
trained lawyer, Gavin Stevens, as witnesses of the Christian claim and hope. The pride of a Southern belle,
Temple Drake, is inexorably probed and sifted by God
and the Devil — we are reminded of Kipling's Tomlin-
son — in a long scene which represents no less than the
threshing out of a naked soul before the divine throne.

The paradox appears in the fact that the instrument of redemption is a Negro Magdalen, drug addict, and household drudge. The import of the whole spiritual transaction is connected with the unlikely human instruments involved. Grace takes on authenticity when its power is manifested among the lost, when daemons are exorcised and hell is harrowed. As Yeats says,

> out of rock,
> Out of a desolate source,
> Love leaps upon its course.[18]

and again,

> Love has pitched his mansion in
> The place of excrement:
> For nothing can be sole, or whole
> That has not been rent.[19]

We learn here to recognize the incognitos of God. Faulkner seems to be saying that there are many nuns not in habits, and many apostles who have not been ordained, and who would not presume. He knows how to present the baneful legacy of a fossilized religion and of a secularized Christian society, but he also can demonstrate the perennial vigor of the faith in redeeming those very ills.

Notes

Notes

I. Religious Dimensions in Modern Literature

Prisoner for God (New York: Macmillan, 1954), p. 167.
L'Art Sacré au XXᵉ Siècle (Paris: Éditions du Ccrf, 1952), p. 149.
1. Wladimir Weidlé, *Les Abeilles d'Aristée* (Paris: Gallimard, 1954), p. 322.
2. *Ibid.*
3. Cited in Father William Tiverton [Martin Jarrett-Kerr], *D. H. Lawrence and Human Existence* (London: Rockliff, 1954), p. 109.
4. Weidlé, p. 322.
5. Ed. by John Heath-Stubbs and David Wright. (London: Faber and Faber, 1953), p. 31.
6. See Will C. Jumper, "Whom Seek Ye? A Note on Robert Lowell's Poetry," *The Hudson Review*, IX, 1 (Spring 1956), pp. 117–125.
7. Tiverton, p. viii.
8. D. H. Lawrence, *The Rainbow* (New York: Random House, Modern Library Edition), p. 263. Cited by Tiverton, p. 116.
9. Gustav Janouch, "Conversations with Kafka," *The Partisan Review*, XX, 2 (March–April 1953), p. 178.
10. Cincinnati: University of Cincinnati Press, 1949.
11. *The American Adam* (Chicago: University of Chicago Press, 1955), p. 56.
12. In *Religious Symbolism,* ed. by Ernest Johnson (New York: Inst. for Religious and Social Studies, 1955), pp. 159–184.
13. See note 11.
14. *Harvard Theological Review*, XLVIII, 4 (October 1955), pp. 239–253.
15. "Offener Horizont und christliche Gewissheit," *Zeitwende: Die neue Furche*, XXVI (January 1954), pp. 21–26.

16. Martin Jarrett-Kerr, *Studies in Literature and Belief* (London: Rockliff, 1954), p. 128.
17. Margaret Crosland, *Jean Cocteau: A Biography* (New York: Knopf, 1956), p. 165.
18. *Prisoner for God* (New York: Macmillan, 1954), pp. 123–124.

II. The Church and the Modern Arts

1. Fritz Eichenberg, *Art and Faith* (Wallingford, Pa.: Pendle Hill, Pendle Hill Pamphlet no. 68, December 1952), p. 7.
2. Howard Schomer, "Barth on Mozart," *The Christian Century,* LXXIII, 29 (July 18, 1956), p. 847.
3. John Betjemen, *Slick but not Streamlined* (New York: Doubleday & Co., 1947), p. 95.
4. See the statement published by the department, "The Church, The Arts, and Contemporary Culture." The department has initiated a society, "Christianity and the Arts Associates." For information as to the department or its commissions on the various arts, address the Department of Worship and the Arts, National Council of Churches, 297 Fourth Ave., New York 10, New York.
5. New York: Harper, 1952.
6. Wallace Stevens, "An Ordinary Evening in New Haven," IX, *The Auroras of Autumn* (New York: Knopf, 1950), pp. 126–127, p. 136.
7. *Ibid.,* p. 111.
8. *Ceremony and Other Poems* (New York: Harcourt, Brace, 1950), p. 5.
9. "Hypocrite Auteur, mon semblable, mon frère," *Collected Poems, 1917–1952* (Boston: Houghton Mifflin, 1952), pp. 173–174.
10. *Nones* (New York: Random House, 1951), pp. 64–70.
11. "Poetry, Religion, and Theology," *Review of Metaphysics,* IX, 2 (December 1955), p. 260.
12. New York: Sheed, 1933.
13. New York: Holt, 1932.
14. New York: Pantheon, 1953.
15. *Essay on Man* (New Haven: Yale University Press, 1944). I owe this citation and the following one to Dr. Walter L. Nathan of Bradford Junior College.
16. "Archaischer Torso Apollos," *Neue Gedichte,* Part II (Leipzig: Insel Verlag, 1908), p. 1.
17. See Martin Jarrett-Kerr, *Studies in Literature and Belief.*

III. Theology and Aesthetic Judgment

Prisoner for God (New York: Macmillan, 1954), p. 94.

1. Introduction to *Charles Péguy: Men and Saints* (New York: Pantheon Books, 1944), pp. 17–18.
2. *Prisoner for God*, p. 115.
3. "An Ordinary Evening in New Haven," XVII, *The Auroras of Autumn*, p. 143.
4. Bern: A. Francke, 1946.
5. *Mimesis*, p. 29.
6. *Ibid.*, p. 76.
7. "Das abendlaendische Geschichtsdenken: Bemerkungen zu dem Buch von Erich Auerbach, Mimesis," *Zeitschrift fuer Theologie und Kirche,* 51 (1954), pp. 270–360.
8. Cited by Lukas Fischer, "Die Rechtfertigung der Schriftstellerei in der alten Kirche," *Theologische Zeitschrift,* XII, 3 (May–June 1956), p. 325.
9. Paraphrase and citation of Wilamowitz-Moellendorff, *Die griechische und lateinische Literatur und Sprache,* pp. 157ff, by R. H. Strachan, *The Second Epistle of Paul to the Corinthians* (London: Hodder and Stoughton, 1935), pp. xxxvii–xxxviii.
10. *The Baptism of Art* (Westminster: The Dacre Press). See review by Georges Florovsky, *Scottish Journal of Theology,* IV (1951), pp. 330–333.
11. What follows on the Fathers is taken from the paper by Lukas Fischer, see note 8.
12. London: Athlone Press, 1950.
13. *Ibid.*, p. 21.
14. Unpublished paper: "Synonyms As Part of the 'Literary' Character of the King James Version."
15. "Under Which Lyre — A Reactionary Tract for the Times," *Nones* (New York: Random House, 1951), p. 70.
16. "Proofs of Holy Writ," *The Strand Magazine* (April 1934); also New York: Doubleday Doran, 1934.
17. *The Common Pursuit* (London: Chatto & Windus, 1952).
18. London: The Sheldon Press, 1940.
19. London: S. C. M. Press, 1949.
20. *The Common Pursuit*, p. 249.
21. *Ibid.*, pp. 252–253.
22. "Poetry and Crisis," *Cross Currents,* no. 4 (Summer 1951), pp. 12–25.
23. *Ibid.*, p. 19.

24. London: Rockliff, 1954.
25. *Ibid.*, p. 164.
26. "A Christian Theory of Dramatic Tragedy," *The Journal of Religion*, XXXI, 1 (January 1951).
27. See Nathan A. Scott, Jr., "Prolegomenon to a Christian Poetic," *Journal of Religion*, XXXV, 4 (October 1955), pp. 191–206.
28. *Poetry and Dogma* (New Brunswick: Rutgers University Press, 1954).
29. As rephrased by John E. Smith, "Poetry, Religion and Theology," *The Review of Metaphysics*, IX, 2 (December 1955), pp. 263–264.
30. See *ibid.*, p. 261.
31. The citations are taken from *Jean Cocteau* by Margaret Crosland (New York: Knopf, 1956), pp. 134–135.
32. "An Ordinary Evening in New Haven," XIII, *The Auroras of Autumn*, pp. 134–135.
33. See D. W. Harding, "Progression of Theme in Eliot's Modern Plays," *The Kenyon Review*, XVIII (1956), pp. 337–360.
34. See John E. Smith, p. 260.
35. See the discussion of modern idealism and solipsism in Nathan A. Scott, Jr., note 27.
36. "Barth on Mozart," *The Christian Century*, LXXIII, 29 (July 18, 1956), p. 847. For the full text see Karl Barth, *Wolfgang Amadeus Mozart 1756/1956*, Zweite Auflage (Basel: Evangelischer Verlag, 1956).

IV. The Cross: Social Trauma or Redemption

The Collected Poems of W. B. Yeats (New York: Macmillan, 1937), p. 246.
New York: Macmillan, 1940. p. 57.
1. Paris: Grasset, 1919.
2. *Dear Judas and Other Poems* (New York: Horace Liveright, 1929).
3. See my previous discussion of Jeffers: "The Nihilism of Robinson Jeffers," in *Spiritual Aspects of the New Poetry* (New York: Harper, 1940). ch. XII.
4. Ann Arbor: The University of Michigan Press, 1956. For Squires' discussion of *Dear Judas* see especially pp. 96, 99–102, 123–125.
5. From the introduction to his volume *The Double Axe and*

Other Poems (New York: Random House, 1948), p. 131. Cited by Squires.

6. *The Selected Poetry of Robinson Jeffers* (New York: Random House, 1938), p. 71.
7. *Roan Stallion, Tamar and Other Poems* (New York: Boni and Liveright, 1925), p. 95.
8. *The Double Axe and Other Poems,* p. 120.
9. *Dear Judas,* p. 48.
10. *Ibid.,* p. 39.
11. "The Theory of Truth," *Selected Poetry,* p. 615.
12. *The Collected Poems of W. B. Yeats* (New York: Macmillan, 1937), p. 215.
13. *Ibid.,* p. 246. Note the context of the lines: a new cycle of ages, a new Magnus Annus, is introduced by the death of Christ. This cycle is marked by "Galilean turbulence." The star of the Magi and the child of the "fierce virgin" initiate a sanguinary age of disorder:

> The Babylonian starlight brought
> A fabulous, formless darkness in.

14. *The Cock of Heaven* (New York: Macmillan, 1940), book VII, iv, p. 57.
15. *Dear Judas,* p. 33.
16. *Ibid.,* p. 38.
17. New York: Dodd, Mead & Co., 1933.
18. *Ibid.,* p. 72.
19. John Mackay, "Miguel de Unamuno," in Carl Michalson, ed., *Christianity and the Existentialists* (New York: Scribner, 1956), pp. 52–53. The references are to Unamuno's essay "The Spanish Christ" (in his volume, *Perplexities and Paradoxes,* 1945) and his poem "The Christ of Velasquez."

V. Faulkner and Vestigial Moralities

The Collected Poetry of W. H. Auden (New York: Random House, 1945), p. 165.

1. One example — Randall Jarrell is speaking of Robert Graves: "Graves says that his religious training developed in him as a child 'a great capacity for fear (I was perpetually tortured by the fear of hell), a superstitious conscience and a sexual embarrassment' " ("Graves and the White Goddess — Part II," *The Yale Review,* XLV, 3, Spring 1956, p. 467).

2. New York: Random House, The Modern Library Edition, 1951, p. 93.

3. *The Sound and the Fury* and *As I Lay Dying* (New York: Random House, Modern Library Edition, 1946).

4. One can apply to her what is said of the Negro servant of Temple Drake in *Requiem for a Nun:* "nurse: guide: mentor, catalyst, glue, whatever you want to call it, holding the whole lot of them together . . . in a semblance at least of order and respectability and peace; not ole cradle-rocking black mamma at all" (New York: Random House, n.d., p. 157).

5. *The Sound and the Fury*, p. 277.

6. *Requiem for a Nun*, p. 135.

7. *The Sound and the Fury*, p. 95.

8. "Moral and Temporal Order in *The Sound and the Fury*," *The Sewanee Review*, LXI (1953), p. 223.

9. *Requiem for a Nun*, p. 92.

10. "Time in Faulkner: *The Sound and the Fury*," in *William Faulkner: Two Decades of Criticism*, ed. by T. J. Hoffmann and O. W. Vickery (East Lansing, Michigan: Michigan State College Press, 1954), pp. 180ff.

11. *The Sound and the Fury*, pp. 142–143.

12. *Ibid.*, p. 10.

13. *Ibid.*, p. 9.

14. *Ibid.*, p. 194.

15. *Ibid.*, p. 312.

16. *Ibid.*, pp. 312–313.

17. *Ibid.*, p. 313.

18. "His Confidence," *The Collected Poems of W. B. Yeats* (New York: Macmillan, 1937), p. 301.

19. "Crazy Jane Talks With the Bishop," *Ibid.*, p. 298.

Index

Index

References in italic type indicate quotation or discussion

143